YOU CONTAIN MULTITUDES

Jayson Iwen

Copyright © 2024 Dr. Jayson Iwen

You Contain Multitudes
Oprelle Publications, LLC

All rights reserved. No part of this publication may be reproduced, distributed, or transmitted in any form by any means, including photocopying, recording, or other electronic methods without the prior written permission of the author, except in the case of brief quotations embodied in reviews and certain other noncommercial uses permitted by copyright law. For information address: Oprelle Publications, 236 Twin Hills Rd. Grindstone, PA 15442.

Cover Illustration by Gregory Klassen

FIRST EDITION
Printed in the United States of America
ISBN: 9798876096333

YOU CONTAIN MULTITUDES

"Clarity about the self dims and brightens like a lamp in a thunderstorm or a radio signal from far away… All those others with me now are a source of identity and partners in my survival."

Mary Catherine Bateson

For my students

Table of Contents

Introduction: The Germ 1
Part I: Strengthening *8*
The Contingency of Identity 12
The Importance of Being Honest 17
Defamiliarization 22
Understanding Inventory 26
The Mansion of Your Self 31
A Haunted Mansion 38
Blame and Sacrifice 43
Futures Inventory 45
Life Maps 48
Narratives We Live By 52
Faith Versus Fate 55
Part II: Stretching *58*
Feeding Your Imagination 62
Embracing Ugliness 67
Your Attention Is Your Life 72
Unsolvable Mysteries 75
Everyday Eternity 78
You Are Everywhere 80
Exposure 84

Systematic Derangement of the Senses 88
The Intelligence of Fire 91
Being Water 93
Being Wild 95
Re-setting Yourself 97
Radical Empathy 101
Memento Mori 103

Part III: Practice *106*

Negative Capability 110
Mental Hierarchies 116
Mind Over Metaphor 123
Defining Yourself 129
Discomfort Zones 131
Covers 134
Making Mantras 137
Audience Awareness 141
Audience Awareness 2.0 146
Identity Dysphoria and De-roling 153
Cracking Your Binary Code 156
Talking to Others 160
Sometimes Love Is the Greatest Challenge 163
Letting Go 165

Conclusion: The Limits of Objectivity 167
Further Study 170
Acknowledgements 173
About the Author 174

Introduction: The Germ

The Kavanaugh hearing completely killed my libido for at least half a year. The combination of Blasey Ford's testimony and the hysterical, infantile outrage of Kavanaugh and certain senators on the Judiciary Committee affected me on such a profound level that I felt disoriented and vaguely ill for days, and when the malaise eventually lifted, my libido went with it. I was no longer able to appreciate the physical beauty of others as I previously had. It was as though, by having been exposed to the grotesque subterranean animus of much of America's current leadership, my revulsion was so thorough that something within me had become diseased and rotted away, leaving a hollow core behind.

Though a semblance of my former sexuality gradually returned by spring, it remained affected. Over the course of the months it was away, I reflected upon its loss. I reflected upon the public display of the hearing, and I concluded that, though I have striven all of my life to be good, a strain of what afflicts those men is possibly within me, whether planted there by our culture in my earliest years or woven into my genetic code before I was even conceived, suppressed to civilized levels perhaps because I experienced domestic violence as a child and tried to avoid it at all costs throughout my life, or perhaps because I had admired Buddhist theology from an early age… perhaps only because something slightly stronger was also woven into my fiber.

Though we will likely never know for sure what makes us who we are, I do know there are practices and beliefs that one can exercise in order to expose unconscious programming and mitigate it, so one may cultivate adaptability, resilience, and personal effectiveness. In a sense, there are ways to true one's internal compass so it aligns with a world that precedes prejudice, a world that can differ greatly from the imaginary or outdated worlds described to us by our cultural influencers and "leaders."

In this book, I present practices drawn from a number of traditions that I have studied over the course of my life so far, particularly from over thirty years of continuous training as a poet. I have found these approaches useful not only for seeing the world in new ways that have resulted in award-winning writing but also for navigating the remarkably different cultural environments where I have lived and worked. For example, during the years that I lived in the Middle East and the years that I taught at an all-Black college in southern Ohio, I found these types of exercises to be useful in maintaining a calm open-mindedness that enabled me to be a happy, productive member of those communities. I continue to practice these techniques to maintain awareness of my own biases, so I am more likely to be in control of them rather than they being in control of me.

I have distilled many of the exercises in this book from my extensive study and practice of the art of poetry.

I have noticed that many of the approaches that make one a better poet also tend to make one a more observant, peaceful, and confident person in general, so I decided to create a systematic program by which anyone can learn and apply these techniques to their own lives. By practicing these techniques as rigorously as one would practice a sport, you will make yourself more successful at breaking out of constraining habits of thought in which you might be caught. Just as artists use such techniques to make innovative new art, you can use them to infuse your life with new potential.

Unconscious bias remains unconscious primarily because it is incorporated into the very fabric of our identities, which we rarely ever examine critically, so we will be turning much of our attention to the nature of identity in this book. However, as important as it is to understand the unconscious power that identity has over us, it is also important for us to remember that no one can transcend identity. Every culture into which we step will have a role ready for us, based on our appearance, our language, and our passport, and we often have no choice but to be cast in that role. However, we do have control over how we play the role. And, most importantly, we know that we are not the role. We are each a being of infinite potential, one that preexists any roles subsequently assigned. Though, in any human society, we must inhabit roles, as an animating spirit inhabits a body, we must always remember that we are not the roles. We are the actor who plays them. And to be a good actor, we must strive to understand all the roles that actors could be asked to perform, though we might personally never be expected to perform many of those roles. We must understand what our fellow actors are asked to do. Only then are we fully aware of what is happening around us.

Poets are concrete philosophers. To practice our art effectively, we cannot work exclusively in domains of only the mind or only the body but must constantly translate between the two, so that our ideas can be felt viscerally. This means that knowledge and understanding must be embodied experiences for us. That's why this book is structured like an exercise manual, to bring mind and body together in the practice of this most challenging of endeavors—understanding self and identity.

The following pages will be divided into three parts: "Strengthening," "Stretching," and "Practice." As in physical training, we first need to make sure we have a strong foundation upon which to build our skills. In the "Strengthening" section, we will work on strengthening our understanding of ourselves and the many different identities that we contain, and we will learn important concepts that will be crucial for our success at the exercises that follow in the later sections. In the "Stretching" section, we will engage in a series of exercises designed to expand or stretch our sense of self. This will make us more flexible and adaptable, so we are less likely to feel injured when one of our identities is challenged. Finally, the "Practice" section will provide us with a series of more challenging exercises designed to build on the gains of the first two sections by cultivating skills and habits crucial for improved interpersonal relations. All the activities in this book are intended to be applicable to anyone of any assigned or assumed identity.

Finally, a note on terminology before proceeding: I will be using the terms "identity" and "role" almost interchangeably throughout this book. Conventionally, "identity" is considered a static concept, something that simply *is* but does not necessarily *do* anything. On the other hand, "role" implies responsibilities and actions that are expected of those who occupy a given role. In a sense, an identity is usually considered a *being*, while a role is considered a *doing*. This is a false distinction. All identities imply specific behaviors, responsibilities, and goals. Of course, they can change over time, through social action and the evolution of culture, but, in any given life, expectations are felt by individuals who are associated with any particular identity.

An identity is a role you play. To illustrate this, consider one of your dominant identities, one that society reminds you of on a daily basis, such as "man" or "woman." What are the expectations and narratives associated with that identity? When do you know that you are "failing" to live up to that role? People agonize daily over their performance of the identities they have been assigned, which is, of course, extremely unhealthy… and, in most cases, entirely unnecessary. Let us now begin to explore how we can avoid such unnecessary agony by strengthening our understanding of how roles and identities function.

Warm-up!

How many different roles do you play in your life? How are you expected to behave in each role? List as many examples as you can think of here:

Part I: Strengthening

My friend, I am not what I seem. Seeming is but a garment I wear—a care-woven garment that protects me from thy questionings and thee from my negligence.

The "I" in me, my friend, dwells in the house of silence, and therein it shall remain for ever more, unperceived, unapproachable.

Khalil Gibran, from "My Friend"

Khalil Gibran, a poet whose life was divided between two countries and two languages, understood the nature of identity well. What he calls "seeming" in the poem "My Friend" is what I call "identity" in this manual. It is a part given to us to play in the grand drama of history. However, it is not who we are when we are born. The "I" Gibran mentions in the poem is who we are when we are born. I call this "I" my "original self," the being who was born into the world and was subsequently assigned and chose identities to embody. This self is the most private and personal part of you, and it is also the most universal, the most like the original self of others.

As Gibran points out, assigned identities protect us from constantly having our motives questioned, because the motives associated with assigned identities are already understood by those around us. The identities existed before we did. Unfortunately, these identities also allow us to be negligent in our behavior toward others, because the identities recommend preexisting courses of action to us, enabling us to not have to make decisions for ourselves. We can simply do what is expected of us by those who are familiar with our identity. However, if one wants to be self-aware, one cannot be negligent in the contemplation of where one's motives originated from and what societal goals they serve.

The exercises in this section are designed to gradually strengthen your understanding of self, identity, and the motives implied by your personal identities. You will also strengthen your understanding of a number of key concepts that you will need to be familiar with in order to successfully conduct the exercises in the "Stretching" and "Practice" sections that follow. For now, let us begin to explore the mansions that are our selves!

The Contingency of Identity

About ten years ago, as I was scheduling a follow-up appointment after a routine outpatient surgery to remove a basal cell carcinoma from my face, I experienced what is medically referred to as a vasovagal syncope, which is to say that my blood pressure dropped precipitously and I lost consciousness with no warning, apparently falling backwards and striking my head on the waiting room floor. Just before it happened, I remember feeling a slight wooziness and standing at the front desk, but the next several minutes simply do not exist in my memory.

Then there was blackness and a small point of light growing in the center of the blackness. As the circle of light widened, two faces appeared within it, with two blue beams rising up toward the faces. That was all there was. That was the entire world and all of history for me, for what felt like minutes, with nothing outside the circle of light, no people, no land, no oceans, no space. Just these two unrecognizable faces. Then knowledge of the wider world began to filter back in. The faces became human. One became a "woman" and one a "man." They both became "white," even "blonde." The blue beams became blue jeans, presumably containing legs within them, slanting upward toward the faces, which now had shoulders and arms and hands attached to them, and in the hands of each of these humans was a foot, a foot where each of the legs terminated. Then, as though returning from far away to the legs and their body, a sense of "I" entered into it, but an "I" utterly devoid of identity. I had no idea where in the world I was or who these people were standing over me, presumably lifting my legs into the air. Was I lying on the ground? Why did they look so concerned? I felt okay, just confused and somewhat... exhilarated by the sudden mystery of everything around me.

As awareness gradually trickled back, I began trying to locate myself within some kind of context. I theorized that perhaps I had over-imbibed and fallen off a bar stool onto my back somewhere in the world, and that these two concerned people were trying to pick me up... by my feet? Then one of the faces started to look familiar. At that point my identity rushed back to me, the context of my current condition, the narrative of how I had arrived there, the roles and responsibilities which I embodied. The identity of the two faces hovering over me, my dermatologist and his assistant, had brought it all back to me. They were elevating my legs to get the blood back into my brain, because I'd probably passed out while wondering why my right eyeball was going numb. Though I was suddenly relieved to know who and where I was, the sense of exhilaration I had felt on the floor lingered. It was the closest thing to complete freedom I could remember feeling. In the time before remembering who I was, I could have been anyone, anywhere in the universe.

This experience illustrated for me, first-hand, how dependent our identities are upon our environment.

The "I" that first returned to me and began trying to solve the mystery of its condition is the closest I can get in an attempt to recognize an original, un-imprinted self. As soon as it began recognizing its surroundings, as if by echolocation, it's culturally and biologically assigned identities began to materialize out of the darkness of oblivion, and with them came memory itself, repopulating my body with the narrative of my life up to that point. It was as if I had re-experienced the identity acclimation process of my entire life, from birth to 35, condensed into the span of a minute or two.

The dependence of our identities upon the environment for definition undoubtedly provides us with an immense evolutionary advantage regarding our adaptability as a species. It shapes us to fit the physical and social environments around us. However, knowledge of this identity dependence upon environment exposes the fundamental falsehood of the belief in individual independence that is a staple of the American identity. We are as independent as we are taught and empowered to be by our childhood environment. Yes, we can transcend that environment, but only if we can find another one that will permit us entrance, even if that environment consists of a remote mountaintop in Montana, for our access to that mountaintop would require sufficient finances for the journey and laws and local communities that permit us undisturbed passage, all of which depends upon our assigned identity.

And if that isn't enough to question one's belief in an individual's independence from its environment, modern science questions the belief that there is even such a thing as an individual. By current estimates, our bodies contain approximately three times more microorganisms than they contain human cells. In other words, what we consider to be our autonomous, inviolable self is actually a massive colony of cohabitating creatures, many of which we could not live without, such as our intestinal bacteria... though many of these creatures could live without us. If we include the identities of these micro-organisms within our currently recognized identities, as it seems only fair to do, then the true picture of your self expands exponentially. The fact that I can have a single thought at a time, when I consist of a multitude of beings, seems truly a miracle. I find it absolutely astounding that there seems to be one self unifying the vast colony of my body, the same self that seemed to fly back to my body from across the universe when my dermatologist and his assistant elevated my legs!

Let's consider one last example of our dependence upon our environments and others. This time our example is a physiological one, though it is also a common subject of meditations across many spiritual traditions: breathing. We cannot choose not to breathe. We have no free will in this regard. Of course, we can take our lives by all sorts of means, but we literally can't decide to do so by consciously holding our breath. Our bodies won't allow it. Our genetic inheritance from our ancestors won't allow it. The world that created our ancestors and their genetic response to it won't allow it. The world is literally making us breathe.

If you are ever feeling lonely, just pay attention to your breathing. Feel all the ancestors in your DNA breathing through you. Feel the trillions of organisms that share your body breathing through you. Feel the entire atmosphere breathing through you. Feel the Earth breathing through you. Feel the Solar System that made the Earth breathing through you, and the universe that made that. The entire history of the universe has resulted in you. It takes a breath when you do. This is as close to your original self as you are likely ever to get.

The Importance of Being Honest

In order for us to benefit from the exercises presented in this book, we will need to be rigorously honest with ourselves about our assumptions and prejudices. Don't worry, you won't need to write anything down or record anything, so no material evidence has to result from the recommendations of this book. It can all remain in your head, as private thought experiments, privy only to you. But no belief, attitude, preference, or priority should remain unexamined in the course of this study of your self. Allow no assumptions about yourself to be beyond questioning.

To help illustrate the importance of full self-disclosure, I'm going to use for an example a subject of tremendous importance that has been brought to the forefront of public attention in recent years. It is the subject of criminality and how mainstream American culture associates it with some identities but not with others. For example, most middle- and upper-class white Americans have been trained from birth to believe that criminal behavior is something to be associated with groups other than middle- and upper-class white Americans. This unconscious cultural programming is so thorough that many don't even believe they are capable of criminal behavior. The threat of becoming a criminal is one they associate almost exclusively with "others," which means just about anyone who isn't a middle- or upper-class white person.

In fact, according to the symbolic logic of mainstream Western culture, many white Americans, including many who consciously detest racism, unconsciously believe that one's likelihood of engaging in criminal behavior increases in direct proportion to how far one's skin tone is away from being bright white. If they see a white teenager walking through a white neighborhood, they think nothing of it, but if they see a black teenager walking through the same neighborhood, they are tempted to dial 911 and report "suspicious behavior." These would-be reporters almost invariably identify themselves as law-abiding citizens, blameless of wrongdoing. These kinds of beliefs about one's identity are too superficial for the purposes of our current endeavor. We would make little progress in an effort at identity detox if we didn't honestly assess such assumptions about our identities. The universal truth is that every one of us, from the perspective of another culture, can be considered guilty of criminal behavior by the standards of that other culture.

But even within our own culture that is often the case. If I were to honestly assess whether or not I, a white American, could fit into the category of "criminal," this very moment, I would first ask myself exactly what a criminal is. A quick glance at any dictionary informs me that a criminal is someone who commits a crime, which requires me to look up "crime," which I am informed is either an act that has broken a law, or it is an "evil, shameful, or wrong" act that hasn't necessarily broken any established laws, implying that the laws themselves might be derelict. So, practicing the kind of honesty necessary for this book to work, I have to admit that I, in fact, could be considered a criminal, by both dictionary definitions, for I do, honestly, commit the kinds of petty crimes that nearly everyone does these days, such as jaywalking, speeding, not coming to a complete stop at stop signs, etc. Just because I don't consider these to be significant crimes doesn't mean they aren't crimes, and it doesn't mean I'm not a criminal. It just means I'm not a convicted criminal.

How do I fit the second definition of "criminal"? Have I done anything "evil, shameful, or wrong"? Well, that depends entirely upon the belief system we apply to my situation. If, for example, my current lifestyle was to be scrutinized a hundred years from now, we can be assured that I would be perceived as having harbored some shameful or wrong beliefs that led to shameful or wrong behavior, just as many of the past's most common beliefs (geocentrism, humorism, phrenology, etc.) are perceived by most of us today. And, of course, in other currently existing cultures, certain behaviors of mine, such as consuming alcohol, for example, are considered criminal. Crime, like motion, is relative to your position in space. So the answer is undeniable: I could easily be considered a criminal, by multiple definitions of the word.

So, why does it matter, in this particular example, that I acknowledge that I could be identified as a criminal in contexts both actual and potential? Because this acknowledgement prevents me from excusing myself from examining a role that I might otherwise assign exclusively to others. If I were to habitually associate that role with others, I would not be understanding the nuances of who I really am, as opposed to who I assume I am. I would likely stop thinking about the role and definition of "criminal" at that point, assuming it bore no relevance to my identity, other than if an actual criminal were to commit a crime against me. I would likely exile all those who have been labeled criminals to another place in my mind, locked away in a room where I put all "others" whom I don't consider to be "like me," a place in my mind I don't visit often, because it seems removed from the daily concerns of my life, which I feel are anything but "other" to me.

In addition to possibly behaving in an inhumane fashion toward others because of these assumptions, I would also be deceiving myself. I wouldn't be treating myself with the common decency of taking myself seriously and respecting the actual conditions of my life. There's no way I could become wiser or more resilient if I began anywhere but with an honest appraisal of my self.

Warm up!

When have you noticed someone making an assumption about someone else? How often were those assumptions accurate and how often were they not? List as many examples as you can think of here:

Defamiliarization

A key practice that we will be returning to periodically throughout this book is "defamiliarization." It is at the heart of all forms of creativity and open-mindedness and thus deserves an introductory explanation before we move on. The process of becoming adapted to environments, both social and physical, requires us to become familiarized with those environments, to come to understand and be able to participate in the behavior of those who occupy those environments, to learn the purpose and conventional use of the tools and practices employed by those people, to adopt the values that allow those people to succeed by their own standards. This is one of the hallmarks of human evolution. We are very adaptable. However, in order for us to be able to be so adaptable, we start life with fewer instincts than other creatures, with fewer biologically ingrained predispositions.

For example, once we are weaned from our mother's milk, our diets veer off toward whatever happens to be edible and available in our surroundings. We model our behavior upon those around us, both consciously and unconsciously, as quickly as we can, to make up for the lack of hardwired instinct. As a species, we gambled on the advantages of culture and education over those of instinct. Unlike cats, for example, we aren't born with a taste for mice and the inherent behavior that makes us likely to find them. We are born with the desire to imitate those around us... and to put everything we can into our mouths!

Through this act of familiarizing ourselves with our surroundings we survive. But, in order for the process to work, we must first be unfamiliar with everything. That's why children are considered both innocent and creative, not because they are any more so than the adults around them, but because they have not yet been fully familiarized with the ways and values of adults, the ones who are showing them how to survive. They are still learning.

When a child first encounters a pen, they only know the shape of the thing. They have no idea what it's "for," what its assigned value and purpose are. It's simply another object to be explored... chewed on, taken apart, etc. Once the purpose of the thing is made clear to them, through instruction and reinforcement and reward, they begin to see it only that way. They move on to the next lesson that will enhance their survival. In this way, we become re-adapted to the environment with each new generation, making us far less likely to be vulnerable to changing environments... within reason, of course, as there are basic physical limitations to what the human body can withstand. And there is a dark side to this process as well...

Humans love to learn. That, at least, is one instinct we are born with, and one which, in our evolutionary past, we usually died with as well, because for millions of years, our ancestors didn't tend to live very long. These days, most of us have thoroughly adapted to our physical and cultural environments by the age of 40. By then we've reached the stage I mentioned above in my pen example, where we have become so habituated to the assigned purpose of things that we have trouble seeing them any other way. It's not a coincidence that many people experience "mid-life crises" after they reach this point. Ironically, this is also when we begin to have the most influence over our surroundings, when we begin to be role models for those going through the familiarization process. If we're not careful, we pass the stagnation on to them.

This is precisely how roles and identities can become rigidly reinforced in cultures that do not have the self-awareness on a societal level to accommodate changing needs. In a sense, that is precisely why I am writing this manual: to offer a way to gain greater self-awareness and adapt to change in a way that humans are predisposed to do from birth. However, to do so as a fully acculturated adult requires some strategic "defamiliarization." We need to revisit some of the unconscious practices we engaged in as children, when we were still profoundly open-minded and in love with learning.

In a nutshell, defamiliarization is a process by which you simply observe an object, action, or role as it is, without attempting to determine the purpose or value of the thing. You banish from your mind the usual purpose you assign to that thing. You pick up the pen and study it, turning it over in your hands, observing its traits, testing its materials however you like, taking it apart, reassembling it in different ways, and you will discover, or rediscover, that a pen can be used for all sorts of other creative purposes, including, but certainly not limited to, launching small projectiles, finger painting, and performing emergency tracheotomies!

Nearly every cutting-edge corporation knows that defamiliarization is one of the keys to innovation, along with daydreaming and cross-disciplinary dialogue, and they often incorporate it into the lives of their employees through such activities as cross-departmental team-building challenges and directed play. However, we will be doomed if we expect corporations to save humanity. We each need to do the work of routine reassessment to keep our collective aim true.

Understanding Inventory

The most important self-awareness strengthening routine for us to do is to conduct a series of personal inventories, to help locate ourselves within the vast web of human concerns. The first inventory will be of our understandings. By an "understanding inventory," I don't mean a catalog of everything we know, which would be too massive and unwieldy to be of much use to us. The meaning of the word "understanding" that I am using here is the one that represents things that make sense to us on a holistic, gut-level: morally, ethically, emotionally, etc., what we mean when we say we understand where someone is coming from. Even this kind of inventory would be difficult for many people to conduct, because the potential list would likely be huge and amorphous, and because we don't tend to consciously think about what we understand. We simply take it for granted, which is precisely why we need to find a way to bring some of these understandings into the light of our self-assessment. Fortunately, there's a trick for doing so.

      The trick is what I call a "negative-identification" method. To find out what we do understand, we can often more easily work backwards from what we don't understand, starting with what we consider the negative of ourselves. This works because the identity of human communities is usually formed in contrast to what is perceived or imagined to be the opposite of those communities, with that opposite usually being an identity that has been assigned to a neighboring or foreign community. However, the immediate purpose of this inventory is not to understand other communities better. The purpose for now is to render more visible to yourself the identity to which you have acclimated yourself, mostly unconsciously, since birth.

This will not be an exhaustive list, but it will be illustrative, if you remember to practice the complete honesty I wrote about earlier. Let's now begin brainstorming things that you don't understand, not gaps in knowledge but things that just don't make sense to you, things that just don't feel right to you. Feel free to begin with topical news of the day. The sensational nature of commercial news lends itself well to this exercise. Commercial news doesn't usually provide explanations for the things people can't "understand," because then the audience would understand the issues and be less likely to stare in horror, utterly entranced by whatever is being sold to them.

I'll provide an example inspired by the news to illustrate how to proceed with this particular exercise. I can easily say I don't understand how someone could blow himself up in a public place with the intent to maim and murder others for the sake of a belief. At this point, for this particular exercise, that's as far as I need to go into what I don't understand. At a later point, I might want to do some background research into this news story, to satisfy my inherent curiosity, but for now I'm merely using this item as a starting point for my personal identity self-assessment. What I want to do now is break down my response to the news story, identifying all of my current "understandings" about the world that make this story particularly unacceptable to me.

First, my initial reaction to suicide is always bad. I've been trained to believe that the voluntary extinguishment of one's self is one of the greatest tragedies imaginable. I know this is not true in all cultures, perhaps not even in most cultures. Nevertheless, that's how I feel, and it feels very personal to me. So that's one of my understandings. Second, of equal strength is my understanding that there is a distinct difference between combatants and noncombatants, and that to attack noncombatants is a crime. This is because combatants have presumably chosen, of their own free will, to participate in mortal combat, while noncombatants have not chosen to do so. They have not chosen to potentially die for a cause.

I realize there is more than a little hypocrisy present in my belief that suicide is wrong yet voluntarily subjecting oneself to potential death is acceptable. I also realize that when I use the word "cause" to describe a belief, dying for it suddenly seems palatable. This exposes another understanding of mine, that sacrifice for a tangible goal is fine, while sacrifice for an intangible goal is not sensible. I reluctantly admit that this might make me more of a materialist than an idealist. I don't usually think of myself that way, but there might be something to it.

I could continue for quite some time with this particular news item, using it to unearth more understandings. If any children died in this attack, it would likely dredge up my understanding that children are more valuable than adults, because of their undefined futures, which I presumably value more than defined futures. It would also expose that I believe children are less capable of making decisions for themselves, meaning they are less responsible for having been present at the tragedy, their deaths therefore more tragic because they didn't exercise free will.

Like I said, I could go on, but I hope the exercise is fairly clear now. Once again, the purpose of this particular exercise isn't to come to an understanding of the suicide bomber's mind but to expose your own inherited and likely contradictory assumptions about the world and to better understand your own mind. Don't restrict yourself to the news. Any kind of behavior that you don't understand is a great place to begin your understanding inventory. Not understanding why a certain neighbor never mows his lawn can be equally as revealing of one's own unique understandings of the way the world is supposed to work... but never does completely... and never will.

Warm up!

Find a news report that surprises you and make a list of all the assumptions you have that make the report surprising to you. Question those assumptions to identify your fundamental understandings of the world:

The Mansion of Your Self

Now that we've primed the pump, it's time to get down to the most basic task necessary before we dig deeper into ourselves. We need to create an inventory of all the different identities that have been assigned to us by others and by ourselves. We tend to have shorthand definitions for ourselves that I have previously referred to as "dominant identities," because they are the ones that are socially valued most. It's important to remember that, because identities exist only in contrast to other identities, dominant identities are also relative, meaning they depend on the social context in which you find yourself. For example, if you are the only apparent female in a room of men, your dominant identity in that moment is that of a woman. You will feel distinctly female, and those around you will most likely think of you that way as well... unless you also happen to be the only American in that room. In that case, "American" will most likely take over as your dominant identity, and you will feel and be thought of primarily through that lens.

Given the current cultural climate in the US, our dominant identities tend to be defined by race, sex, and gender. Of course, these are absolutely crucial identities to examine, but we need to understand that they are also part of a much bigger picture. We have to dig deeper into identity if we are to make any kind of meaningful progress in our task at hand. The web of human identification is so complex that it would be nearly impossible to create a comprehensive list of all the identities that intersect at the point of your personal being, so, once again, this will not be an all-inclusive list, but we do want it to be as robust as we can make it with the time we have.

If you find it challenging to move beyond the dominant identity that is routinely applied to you the most by society, try using the negative-identification method I discussed in the last chapter, as that is often how our identities are instilled in us as children. Being perfectly honest with yourself, begin compiling a list of identities and roles that do not apply to you, groups of people that you do not believe you belong to. Start anywhere.

You can literally look around your immediate physical environment to begin. For example, even though I am currently sitting in a library as I write this, I glance around and see a young, ostensibly male student studying behind me. I'm not young. I'm middle-aged. I'm not a student. I'm a teacher, which also makes me an "authority." He's wearing a Red Sox baseball cap. Not only am I not a Rex Sox fan, but I'm also not even terribly interested in baseball beyond the anthropological study of its culture, at least, and I don't identify with Boston, New England, or the East Coast, though I do realize I'm a "Yankee" and could never shake that identity, no matter how long I might live in The South. He's got a crew-cut. I've got long hair. What does that suggest about my likely political persuasion? This library is located on the campus of a Catholic university. Without asking him, I can't be certain of the student's religious beliefs, but I do know I'm not Catholic. I was raised by an Atheist and a Protestant. For hundreds of years in Europe, my association with those identities alone could have prevented me from being permitted into this library... at best.

Speaking of Europe, let's move on to some additional types of identities we can consider. What are the global identities in which I partake? American, third-generation American, North American, former expatriate, native English-speaker, second-language Spanish-speaker, etc. I could go on almost endlessly without having yet touched upon the most common contemporary delineators of identity in America, and yet these are all identities of critical importance, some of which could even put my well-being in jeopardy, in certain places, were I not sensitive to the implications of those identities in those contexts.

To help you structure your inventory a bit more, here is a partial list of some of the more common ways that people identify themselves on a daily basis: by belief (religion, philosophy, theories, etc.), work, politics, physical traits, dress, style, ethnicity, regional affiliation, language, illness, food, pets, hobbies, habits, fears, family roles, relationship status, sports, music, personality, zodiac signs, etc. A comprehensive list is simply not possible. A diagram illustrating the overlap of all the identity groups that contain you would require so many circles that it would be almost impossible to read.

For an example, below is a crude Venn diagram that outlines only three of the most basic aspects of my identity (race, family role, and regional affiliation). "I" am the odd shape at the center, where all the circles overlap.

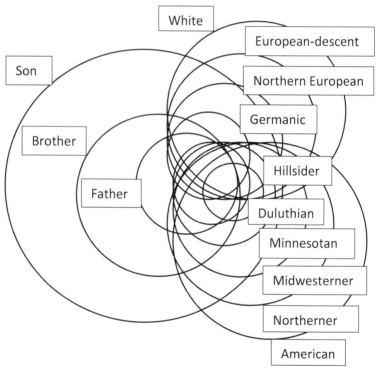

If you are ever feeling lonely or beleaguered, just consider all the other people who share an identity group with you but whom you rarely think about because that identity is not considered important by mainstream society. If it's an important identity to you, it's an important identity. In fact, a powerful exercise is to think of a person whom you consider to be a member of an "other" group, preferably one conventionally considered antagonistic to a group with which you are identified. Then recognize other identity groupings that are important to you and that you also share with that person. Do you share the same sex, gender, nationality, religion, region of residence, hobbies, etc.? Consider the challenges and pleasures that this other identity causes you both to share. Dwell on those for some time. You will feel a door open to a neglected room within the mansion of yourself.

Here's another way you can structure your identity inventory, to help reveal roles you might otherwise miss. You can use the following questions to delve deeper into certain aspects of identity: What roles have you adopted voluntarily and why? What roles have been assigned to you involuntarily and how do you feel about that? Do you feel the way you think you're supposed to feel about your assigned roles? How do you think others feel about their assigned roles? Are there other identities you'd like to have and why? What identities have you had in the past that you no longer have and how do you feel about that? Spend some time with each of these questions and remember to be completely honest with yourself.

There's one final wrinkle we can add to this activity that might be particularly revealing for you. So far we have been expanding our sense of self by cataloguing the manifold identities actively and passively implicated by the circumstances of our birth and the subsequent decisions made by ourselves and those around us. Now let's try moving in the opposite direction of expansion for a bit. Let's practice some minimalism. Consider which of the many identities associated with you is the one you could not live without. If all your roles but one had to be changed, which is the one you would choose to remain part of your new identity? For example, would you trade everything but your occupation? Or everything but your gender? Your race? Your nationality? You might be surprised by what this exercise reveals.

A colleague recently confessed to me that he was considering leaving education to start a private practice in his field, but when faced with the prospect of no longer teaching, he suddenly felt a great unease descend upon him, and he realized that the role of a teacher was too integrally woven into his identity for him to be able to extricate it from his life.

Once you have a decent sense of the complexities and the priorities of your identity composition, we can begin the actual work of figuring out what motivates you unconsciously, providing you with greater agency over your own behavior. We might even begin to figure out who you actually are…

A Haunted Mansion

Now that we've had some practice exercising complete honesty with ourselves and have started taking a closer look at our identities, which are beginning to resemble rambling mansions more than the cozy bungalows we may have initially imagined them to be, we should be ready to enter some of the previously avoided or unexplored rooms of that estate.

Our next inventory will be an inventory of fears, but not the types of fears people usually talk about, such as spiders and snakes and heights. What we're most interested in revealing for the purpose of our identity detox are the fears we harbor about other groups of people, those who are not part of our identity groups... or, more accurately, those people who are not part of the identity groups we are told by our communities to value the most, the groups who threaten the identity of your group the most in your mind. Of course, we will keep in the back our minds the knowledge that every member of a group you fear is also a member of at least one other group with which you are affiliated, but for now we need to expose your fears.

If a group of people associated with a fear doesn't immediately leap to mind, the news is a good place to start, as usual. Again, I can't emphasize how important it is to proceed with intrepid honesty. No one else will need to know what's going through your mind as you perform this exercise. What matters is that you are paying close attention to what is going through your mind. First, pick a group of people that has been presented to you as having suspicious motives, perhaps even presented explicitly as being a threat to your "way of life." The next step is to answer the following questions.

First, what is the dominant identity that has been assigned to this group by the mainstream culture where you live? Try to drill down and be as specific as possible. For example, if "immigrants" came to mind, what kind of immigrants (illegal, legal, naturalized, etc.) and from which regions or nations? Once you've narrowed the group down to a point as close to a fear as you can get, you need to ask yourself exactly what it is that you fear they will do to you. Remember, the purpose of this exercise isn't to overcome your fears. The purpose is to understand your identity better and how it interacts with the identities of others. To do that, you need to be as specific as possible with the scenario or scenarios you imagine in this part of the exercise.

If, for example, you think Mexican immigrants are going to steal your job, you need to conjure that fear and study it. Imagine yourself at your actual workplace. How exactly is this scenario going to most logically unfold? Go through it as realistically as you can imagine it would proceed. How would it happen? What person or group would be responsible for making the decision? Who would you be most upset with in the scenario? How would you feel in that moment? Incidentally, keep in mind that you're not making this scenario up on the spot. It has been playing itself out unconsciously in your mind for some time now, just not very articulately, because you probably haven't trained the spotlight of your consciousness on it until now.

      Okay, now you can pull back from the imagined scenario. If you want, you can assure yourself that it is statistically unlikely to happen to you, as almost all such fears are. But, hold on to the feeling you had in your scenario. If you realized you're more afraid of your boss than of Mexican immigrants, maybe you need to start over with a different group. However, if your feelings were still directed at the original group, hang on to those feelings and take them to a new scenario. This time, imagine a member of that group trying to open a door with a bag of groceries in each arm, while you are standing behind them. What are you going to do in this scenario? And, more importantly, how is your behavior going to likely make them want to behave the next time they see you? How are they going to talk to their children about you? How are they going to want to behave the next time they see someone they associate with your identity? How is it going to affect that other person they associate with you? And on and on…

      Just as the concept of "cold" can't exist without the concept of "heat," there's not a single identity that can exist without the presence of other identities to define it by contrast. This also means that when another identity changes, so do all others that come into contact with it. If a group with which you are associated decides to declare another group an enemy, with or without your consent, your group has just redefined the identity of the other group to include the following trait: it now has your group as an enemy. Everyone on both sides is implicated, willingly or unwillingly, and will be treated accordingly for generations, until more generous spirits prevail in the process of constructively redefining those identities once again.

You should conduct this exercise with every group you associate with a fear, no matter how big or small the fear. If it's possible, create at least one realistic scenario for each fear, mentally record the feelings elicited by the scenario, and forecast how the expression of that feeling would influence the behaviors of both groups towards one another.

I will add one additional visualization to this exercise: consider the logical conclusion of an escalation of aggressions between your group and the group associated with your fear. This new vision should always be your greatest preventable fear.

Warm up!

Make a list of all identity groups that you suspect might feel uneasy around identity groups with which you are associated:

Blame and Sacrifice

Fear is usually followed by anger, especially when we feel that our roles are being questioned or when we are frustrated in our efforts to meet the expectations of those roles, ironically often even for those roles that have been imposed upon us, but certainly for those that we have chosen to embody. And with this anger inevitably comes blame. Due to the interdependent nature of human identities, everyone can be blamed for something, including ourselves, of course. Blame is the most common distraction from self-awareness. The way most people unconsciously practice blame seems to align with theories of limited good. If one believes there is a limited amount of good possible in the world, then one will intentionally sacrifice things currently considered good in the hope of gaining more good in an imagined future. For example, to assure that it will rain, someone who believes in limited good might make a sacrifice to whatever entity they believe controls the currency of good. In this mindset there is also the fear that any good occurrence will eventually be offset by something bad.

Blame tends to work the same way in practice. If some group is perceived to be at blame, then all attention is on them, as they are perceived to be in possession of all of that limited commodity. If blame is assigned, then no one else is guilty. According to this primitive logic, sacrificing that group uses up all the evil, and no further evil will accrue for a while. Some balance between the limited amounts of good and evil is felt to have been achieved, no disasters will occur now. But plate tectonics and weather and guilt don't work this way. Infinite good is possible, as is infinite evil, infinite blame, infinite guilt, and infinite innocence. It is entirely up to us to define what we mean by these qualities and to decide how much we want them to define us. There is no predetermined quantity of any of them in reality. We have the free will to determine that for ourselves.

The first step in this process is, as usual, to look closely at ourselves and the identities with which we are associated. Regarding blame, we need to honestly acknowledge all the ways that we blame other groups, as well as all the ways that other groups might blame us, both legitimately and illegitimately. Make a list of all the things you accuse other identity groups of and make a list of everything your different identity groups have been accused of. This will render more visible to you the web of competing values of which your society is composed and where in that web you are currently caught.

Futures Inventory

What are the different ways that you imagine the future? If you haven't seriously imagined what you think life on Earth will be like by the end of your lifetime, it would be good for you to spend a little time doing that now. Our often unconscious and unarticulated assumptions about the future define our notions of progress and what we perceive to be the obstacles to that progress, obstacles that are often imagined to be other groups of people. When you perform this exercise, you will very likely have two different visions of the future fairly quickly present themselves to you, as provided by popular media: a utopian one and a dystopian one. A realistic vision is far more challenging to imagine, but it is worth the effort to do so. The exercise will present to you a fairly accurate manifestation, or landscape, of your current identity, with your fears and hopes imbedded within it.

Again, the purpose of this inventory is not to predict the future. The future never turns out exactly the way anyone expects it to, as illustrated nicely by nearly all science fiction predictions of the 21st century. The purpose of this inventory is to provide another way to render visible your assumptions about how the world works. It also allows you to more clearly identify how your visions of the future influence your daily behavior. For example, your current occupation is very likely a symptom of your vision of the future of life on Earth. It is your way of preparing. The daily decisions you make, the friendships you forge or forgo, are all linked to these persistent competing visions of the future that you unconsciously maintain, often veering between the visions of your own personal utopia and dystopia. Pause throughout the day to ask yourself how what you are doing at the moment serves one or more of your visions. You will find it an excellent way to put your behavior in perspective, and sometimes you'll even realize that what you are doing is serving no purpose whatsoever.

Once you have a fairly good sense of your competing visions of the future and how they influence your behavior, the next step is to remind yourself that none of these visions will ever come to be as you have envisioned them. The only thing you can be certain of is that the world will change. You will change. Others will change. All forms of human civilization will change. The Earth itself is, of course, constantly changing. Though nearly all assumptions can be thrown out, the inevitability of change is one you need never abandon.

Finally, you can take this thought experiment one step further by turning around and looking behind you. What alternate pasts could you have had and what alternate presents, if you had entered this world under different circumstances, the same exact "you," what you feel to be your quintessential self, your personality and predispositions, but in different contexts. For example, what if you had been born into a different class, race, region, sex? How would this have changed where you are now? Imagine being a child in one of your neighbor's homes. How would your vision of the future likely be different? This step of the exercise will allow you to draw back even further from your personal assumptions, providing you with a broader perspective on the market of human futures.

Life Maps

Before we dive into practices designed to recalibrate fundamental beliefs, there is some additional groundwork we should do. We should first locate the maps we use to navigate our lives. What I mean by a map here is an interconnected system of assumptions we lay over the world before us in order to elicit sets of choices and highlight preferred decisions. The futures I wrote of in the last chapter are part of a map of yours. If we aren't consciously aware of the maps we are using, we can't update them or replace them with more useful ones. These behavioral maps are usually a complex combination of interrelated, learned concepts that often seem open-ended and vague individually, but become powerfully prescriptive when combined and morally weighted to suggest the socially condoned choice of action in any scenario that seems to match the contours of the map. These maps show us the paths society expects us to follow, paths that, over time, become ruts.

I'll provide a simplified version of a map consisting of six concepts that are so common they seem unremarkable, but when combined, whether consciously or unconsciously, they become a map that generations of people worldwide have followed to the end of their lives, many happily so and many in misery, due to reasons often beyond their control, the premier among those reasons being that the latter were following a map incompatible with their character. Here's this particular map: 1) hard work results in success; 2) success leads to wealth; 3) wealth provides security; 4) security permits one to raise a family; 5) a family is a great source of happiness; 6) happiness is the goal of life. When arranged in this order, the course of action suggested by these related concepts becomes obvious.

What should also become obvious, upon reflection, are the many ways in which someone's life narrative could be forced away from this generic, prescribed course, which doesn't take into account basic factors such as class/caste systems, systematic racism and sexism, sexual orientation, addiction, market "downturns," family feuds, laws actually prohibiting certain people from achieving the stated goals, personal definitions of success that aren't valued by mainstream society and thus don't result in financial gain, etc. In fact, when you think about it, it is more surprising when someone achieves the goal than it is when they wander, or are led, astray. Nevertheless, those who become "lost" often feel tremendous guilt for having become so. They feel they have let the world down by failing to achieve what was expected of them. Or worse yet, they are filled with an existential revulsion at society for having hypocritically presented them with ideals that, in practice, it strove to prevent them from realizing.

It is crucial to point out here that any given map is just one of infinite ways to describe the cultural landscape around us and our relation to it. Actual, physical maps, which our behavioral maps resemble on more than a metaphoric level, serve specific purposes for specific audiences. They highlight one or two aspects of a landscape and remove all others. In a sense, they reveal through erasure. Road maps, for instance, shows us roads. They do not show us where we are likely to find gold or oil or a good steak or shade on a hot day. They show us where we can drive cars... assuming we have cars, the resources to fuel and maintain them, driver's licenses, passports, visas, desires to go where the roads lead, etc. Every map is a simplification of the world into a set of concepts supported by innumerable assumptions.

So, before we can do serious work on ourselves, we need to find the maps that guide us through our days. Pay attention to the decisions you make daily and ask yourself which maps are presenting you with your options and suggesting preferred outcomes. By studying our maps we can figure out the purposes the map makers intended for the map, and we can figure out our intended role in that purpose. We can also figure out what is being hidden in order to highlight that purpose. But most importantly, for the purposes of this book, which is itself a new kind of map, I acknowledge, once we identify our habitual maps, we can use them to identify ourselves. We can pinpoint ourselves on the maps, and we can imagine where we might appear in the maps of others.

Warm up!

Pay attention to the decisions you make today. List the assumptions that lie behind the choices you make, as well as the assumptions that would support the alternatives that you do not choose:

Narratives We Live By

One of the most common ways maps are acquired is through narrative. There are a relatively small number of socially accepted genres of life story that are taught to us when we are young and subsequently exert tremendous influence over our behavior by defining the limits of social expectation. The fact that they are learned does not diminish the feeling that our life stories are authentically and spontaneously woven from the fabric of personal experience. Nevertheless, like other maps, they are also incredibly simplified and partial versions of reality. Every culture has life narrative genres unique to that culture as well as genres influenced by other cultures or related by common cultural ancestry. One of the most common of these narratives in America is the "rags-to-riches" narrative that has driven decision-making for countless generations, leading some disadvantaged Americans to actual wealth and many to feelings of abject failure, because the back-breaking labor that forms the backbone of the narrative is not sustainable for your average person and is healthy for almost no one.

    Other common narratives in America would include the likes of "the prodigal son/daughter," a life story of reckless youthful behavior followed by repentance, enlightenment, and often attempts to convert others to one's new lifestyle. There are also narratives of pious, life-long self-sacrifice and misunderstood or unrecognized genius. The "true love" narrative, often in combination with the self-sacrifice narrative, guides many lives, as does the narrative of the imperiled community, with its cast of rough but ultimately saintly defenders. To get a sense of the range of narratives that unconsciously guide us, scrolling through film categories in Netflix or Amazon will conjure more in your mind. In almost all, the good win and the bad lose, and the two are easily distinguishable. Mysteries are solved, and the innocent are vindicated, as is rarely the case in reality.

    I've chosen these examples because they are the most common, the most mainstream, the most likely to be internalized by members of the dominant culture. There are other narratives that exist in subcultures, often designed to be more attainable within the confines of those cultures, but they are usually internalized just as unconsciously and uncritically as the mainstream narratives, received from elders and peers and the cultural productions of the community. In fact, they are often variations of the mainstream narratives, such as the variation of the rags-to-riches narrative that begins with petty theft and, through hard work, intelligence, bravery, and ruthlessness, results in the protagonist becoming a crime lord.

    In order to strengthen one's identity awareness, it is critically important to conduct an inventory of all the narratives that influence one's behavior. I would recommend starting by simply listing all the types of life stories that you are aware of, such as the examples I described earlier. Then I would go through that list and identify the narratives that have the most emotional appeal to you. These are probably the ones that unconsciously guide you more than others, even if the decisions they lead you to make seem mundane in comparison to the more dramatic decisions made by the protagonists of those tales. You must be aware of this influence if you want to have a less influenced, more objective view of reality. It's also very important to remember that, although some details of these narratives might resemble the actual details of your life, the arrangement of those details, the value placed upon them, and the portrayed outcomes could all occur in an infinite variety of ways, if you choose to become the author of your own story.

    It's hard to change one's own life story if it seems to be following an inevitable path laid out for you by fate. We have to remember that these narratives are not fate. They are stories you were told over and over until you began telling them to yourself to explain the meaning of your life. Once you understand the ultimate arbitrariness of the stories, you can more freely customize yours to suit your personal desires, your unique environment, your actual life.

Faith Versus Fate

What I mean here by "faith" is a forward-leaning belief in the perceived truth of something, meaning that this truth will eventually lead to an outcome you consider inevitable, if you continue to behave in accordance with that faith. Though personal agency can certainly influence faith, it is often inherited with assigned or assumed identities. It is a component part of what we call identity. Therefore, to better understand and control our identities, we need to understand our faiths.

First, you should conduct a faith inventory by making a list of all the things in which you have faith. When you're done with that, look over your list and consider the faiths that counter yours. Consider faiths that are entirely absent from your list and those not even implied by it. For example, if you have faith that humans can ultimately overcome any challenge through technological innovation, imagine an alternate to that faith, such as the belief that not all challenges can be overcome through technology and that humans will ultimately need to change their current behavior in order to survive. It's very likely these days that someone might glance over their list and realize that, by omission, they apparently don't have faith in such things as the inherent goodness of humanity, democracy, America, civilization, etc. As always, be completely honest with yourself, and make note of these observations. It's okay not to have faith in things, but you should be aware of it.

The next steps of this exercise constitute a thought experiment of critical importance. Select one of those alternate or absent faiths and consider how you would feel about yourself if you were to have that faith. Would you consider yourself weaker, less intelligent, naïve, etc.? Would you feel that you were causing damage to the world somehow? Again, be perfectly honest with yourself and make note of everything you would feel about yourself if you were to have that faith. Do this with as many of the alternate or absent faiths suggested by your list.

Finally, you should make a list of all the things you wish you could have faith in, and one at a time, work your way through that list and ask yourself the same questions you asked about your alternate and absent faiths. You'll find that the line of questioning will assume a new emotional angle. You will have to consider why you do not allow yourself to have faith in these things. How would you feel about yourself? How might your behavior change? What good might result from such faiths? If you can see no possible good, then what harm do you foresee coming to you or those around you if you have faith in those beliefs? What exactly is holding you back? These are not rhetorical questions. You need to know precisely why you do not have faith in things that you wish you could have faith in, because, if you don't, you are not in charge of your own life—you have been hijacked by an identity, and you need to know that.

You also need to know that faith is a choice, not a fate assigned to you.

> **Warm up!**
>
> What are some fundamental things you believe in, as well as some you wish you could believe in and why you feel you can't:

Part II: Stretching

The Self-Unseeing

Here is the ancient floor,
Footworn and hollowed and thin,
Here was the former door
Where the dead feet walked in.

She sat here in her chair,
Smiling into the fire;
He who played stood there,
Bowing it higher and higher.

Childlike, I danced in a dream;
Blessings emblazoned that day;
Everything glowed with a gleam;
Yet we were looking away!

Thomas Hardy

In "The Self-Unseeing" Thomas Hardy presents us with a poignant illustration of a regret commonly shared by many later in life. In the poem, he visits his childhood home, which seems to have been abandoned for some time, and he remembers a scene from childhood: his mother contentedly sitting by the hearth, listening to his father play the fiddle, while he, as a child, danced to the music. In reflection, he now realizes what a blessing it was for them to have had that evening together, but at the time they didn't realize the significance of what probably felt like a routine to them. In the last line, he proposes what he considers to be the reason they didn't value the experience as much as they should have: they weren't seeing the experience. They were looking elsewhere in their minds.

His title provides us with a further clue to understanding his thinking on the subject. He suggests that they were not recognizing their selves. When we fixate on any one of our identities, this will happen. Our vision narrows to include only the concerns and goals of that particular identity. We lose sight of the much broader vision presented to our original self at birth. In fact, we risk losing sight of that very self, as the self begins to resemble nothing more than a single identity. We can become self-unseeing.

Fortunately, we can do something to prevent this from happening. Now that you've done a number of exercises designed to strengthen your understanding of identity, the next stage in your workout is to stretch what have likely become habitual assumptions about your self and your purpose in life, to push outward the boundaries of what you consider possible. The following exercises are designed to help you expand your sense of self so that you can consciously summon the greater mental flexibility of your childhood years, without compromising the knowledge you have gained since then.

Feeding Your Imagination

The most powerful tool humans possess is our imagination, the nature of which is ultimately fairly simple, but out of that simplicity arises infinite complexity. To understand the nature of imagination, it is helpful to consider the etymology of the word itself, as it nicely captures the spirit of the process that is imagination. "Imagination" comes from the Latin "imaginari," which means to summon an image within one's mind, in the absence of external presentations of that image.

Essentially, imagination is the ability to see what is not present, to see something that might potentially exist in the spatial or temporal distance beyond sight. When we speak of someone being a visionary or "having a vision," we are invoking the same understanding of the process by which imagination operates. In addition to seeing what has existed or what does currently exist in actuality, a visionary is able to produce an alternative model of reality as it might exist. They can see potentiality. They have "imagination." Of course, this is something we all have. The simple act of reading requires one to imagine things that aren't actually physically present, such as the fireplace in Hardy's poem.

Conventional approaches to imagination usually consist of unreflective praise for the importance of it, often followed by suggestions for how to cultivate it.

Imagination is, indeed, a subject of immense significance, but not just because it can lead to happiness and innovation. It is even more important than its enthusiastic admirers think, because it can also lead to misery and devastation. As I said earlier, the imagination is a tool, like fire or language or a hammer, and, like any tool, its design does not determine the ends it will serve. Hammers, for example, are useful for building both homes and gallows. The atomic bomb was the work of imagination.

Imagination is not inherently good or bad. It just is. How it is used is determined primarily by what it is fed. That is the only sensible approach for a highly adaptable species. If one lives in an environment that provides a steady diet of violence, one's imagination will be preoccupied imagining potential sources of violence and ways to deal with it. If one lives in an environment that prioritizes technological innovation by rewarding behavior that results in it, one will likely spend a lot of time imagining ways to advance the capabilities of technology. When one becomes habituated to a particular kind of imagining, it usually happens at the expense of other forms of imagining; they are pushed out of the frame of one's worldview.

For example, a brilliantly competitive businessman might find it almost impossible to imagine ways to compromise and cooperate with others. That's not what he spends his days imagining. Should he care if he's not able to imagine anything else? Well, if he wants to be more fully aware of the human condition and how his life relates to that bigger picture, he should care. But there's another reason he should care. When you anticipate the future, you do so by projecting onto it a vision of your current concerns, and you begin to behave in anticipation of that imagined future. This approach can be a very effective way to prepare for natural events such as food scarcity or inclement weather, but when it is applied to human behavior it can easily backfire because it doesn't take feedback into consideration.

What I mean by "feedback" is the act of interpreting the actions of others and adjusting one's own behavior in response, a response which is then interpreted by those others and leads to an adjusted response to your response, often resulting in a feedback loop that can easily spiral out of control. If, for example, you suspect that someone is "out to get you," you will likely behave toward them in a suspicious fashion that makes them... well, suspicious of you. They will likely begin to suspect that you are out to get them, and they will likely start behaving in ways that reinforce your initial suspicion, further entrenching your position and emboldening your subsequent reactions to their behavior, causing them to do the same. These scenarios don't usually end well. The only ways to pull out of such a nosedive are for a mediator to intercede, for a greater disaster to dwarf the conflict, or for one of the parties to suddenly gain objective self-awareness and open an honest dialogue with the perceived opponent. Of these three, the first option is the most likely to occur. Unfortunately, such nose dives are also just as likely to either continue in seemingly endless conflict or to end with the permanent departure of one of the aggrieved parties.

Fortunately, there are ways to completely avoid negative feedback loops like the one just described. Many of the techniques discussed later in this book will help you do just that. The one I will end this chapter with is one that utilizes your imagination. As with several other techniques covered in this section, it will sound quite simple, but it requires a change of habitual behavior, which makes it a bit more challenging in practice. Essentially, what you need to do is feed your imagination a balanced diet, so you can stop imagining the same scenarios all the time. If one wants to "be more fully aware of the human condition and how your life relates to that bigger picture," one needs to be able to imagine a variety of potential outcomes to any given situation, outcomes that others might imagine, and the best way to do this is to subject yourself to products of imagination that you usually ignore.

If, for example, you subject your imagination to a steady diet of murder mysteries, you should vary that diet, perhaps with some comedy or romance or history or poetry or, really, anything else, to break yourself of the unconscious habit of assuming that everyone around you is a potential suspect in a murder case. If you subject your imagination to a steady diet of tragedy, ditto.

Comedy, ditto. If you find yourself voraciously consuming news, particularly from a single news source, you definitely need to diversify your media diet. The news presents an infinitesimally small sliver of the vast reality of lived human experience—to confine your imagination to that tiny, blood-splattered room is a tragedy of Shakespearean magnitude. If you stay there long enough, you will never be able to leave. Your imagination will simply not be able to fathom what could be outside those walls.

In short, give your imagination more colors to work with when you ask it to paint a picture of the future for you. If you don't, you're likely to end up with nothing but black and white photocopies of the past. Eventually, your own identity could begin to feel hopelessly monochromatic as well.

Embracing Ugliness

It's possible to walk into nearly any neighborhood of any American city and accurately diagnose the political inclinations of that neighborhood based solely upon landscaping. Yards that have been meticulously trimmed and pruned and doused with herbicides and fertilizers, so nothing unintentional remains, are almost assuredly the yards of conservatives, while yards that seem to have been left to their own devices, with unkempt grass harboring weeds, and trees and bushes that appear to have been neglected since the previous owners moved out, are most likely the yards of liberals or independents.

This is not to say that one's taste in landscaping results from one's political persuasion. On the contrary, it is more likely that one's aesthetic sensibilities inform one's politics. Civilizations are defined ultimately by their sense of beauty, by their "taste." Consider their landscapes, their architecture, their art, music, clothing, hair styles, even the preferred attributes of their bodies. What they consider beautiful is what they want to be. And what they consider ugly is what they want to suppress, and they want to do so at such a fundamental level that they don't often realize that the instinct to suppress is based on their sense of beauty, one that was learned at a young age, often arbitrarily determined by the people and the environment around them when they were young.

Curiously, though your sense of beauty, to a great extent, defines your daily life, your beliefs and your ambitions, and thus your life story, your sense of beauty can tell you very little about who you could have been without it. It is almost useless as a tool for understanding the true self, the you before you were trained to recognize "beauty." In the endeavor to render our unconscious prejudices visible, to gain greater self-awareness, we fortunately have the incomparable tool of ugliness.

There are several important points to make about ugliness. First, to remove it from the world you would have to remove the world from existence. It is what defines your beauty, what holds it together by providing contrast. Consequently, you yourself are defined by it; the way a photograph emerges from a film negative. If one does not understand how one's actions are permitted by the suppression of other potential actions that would lead to something ugly, one will never understand the vast majority of one's submerged identity or how one could gain greater control of that identity. Finally, it is crucial to acknowledge that there is nothing in the world that is either inherently beautiful or inherently ugly. It is all relative to one's species, one's environment, one's culture. A sunny day in an otherwise overcast climate would be considered beautiful by most humans, because of certain physiological human needs, but a sunny day in the desert is something else entirely for humans and could easily become a horrifying experience for the unprepared. A pile of excrement is not generally considered beautiful, unless you are one of many species that thrive on it, or perhaps if it is horse manure and you are a gardener.

One's definition of ugliness is anything but universal, even amongst only humans. Barring understandable aversions to life-threatening things, like a bowl of pecans placed before someone with nut allergies, the vast majority of definitions of "ugly" are arbitrarily imposed upon us. I say "arbitrary" from an objective perspective. From the perspective of those imposing the standards of beauty upon you, they are not arbitrary. They are strategically designed to serve the agenda of those in power. What one considers ugly is really a weakness within oneself. It is a limitation, a handicap, that has been placed upon you to prevent you from exploring other ways of being. It is what removes the "innocence" from a child.

So, how do we undo this process? As with snake bite, the anti-venom is most effectively derived from the venom itself. In this case, by confronting what disgusts us, we liberate ourselves from its power over us. Defamiliarization is the key, and the easiest way to achieve defamiliarization, in regard to this subject, is by subjecting yourself to the object of your disgust for so long that it begins to lose its definition in your mind, like the pre-adolescent pastime of saying a word over and over until the end and beginning of the word begin to blur together and it starts sounding like an alien language. If, for example, the color pink irritates you, stare at it, focusing on nothing but the color, until it seems that there is nothing in the world but the color pink and you. When you finally look away, you will be refreshed, and the color pink will no longer have as much power over you.

    This is not the same as desensitization. It is actually enhancing your senses. Staring at a pile of garbage until it is no longer disgusting does not mean you will suddenly feel fine living in a world of garbage. It means you will begin to see what is actually in the garbage. You will not turn away from it in disgust, forcing yourself to ignore it, pushing it out of your consciousness. You will see what is causing the smell. You will see how much of it was reusable or compostable or recyclable. You will see something you were looking for and thought was lost.

    One of the greatest responsibilities of a poet is to recognize beauty in previously unexpected places, to find new sources of pleasure in a changing world and to convey those new forms of beauty to others, so they too can begin to see more beauty in the world, making their days into works of art. But you don't need to be a poet to do this for yourself. An exercise like this one can allow you to, if not open doors to more beauty, at least ease the grip ugliness has on your heart.

> **Stretch!**
>
> Focus on something you find truly ugly. Then make a list of at least ten aspects of it that you can appreciate:

Your Attention Is Your Life

Your predominant identity has been shaped and is reinforced daily by what you are told to pay attention to, by those who hold the most influence over you. Once our system of values is firmly established, usually by late childhood, those values don't need to be reinforced because they are already filtering what our perceptions allow us to experience of the world. As with a map, we begin to see only the things we were taught to value. Everything else has faded into the "background" of the map. Even now, if you look up from these words and glance around you, certain things will attract your attention, not because they are inherently any more important than anything else around you, but because they have been linked to the plot of your life's narrative up to this point. And since you have either directly or indirectly chosen to read this book, I'm guessing that you have had moments when the plot of your life has felt like an endless corridor. If so, what you should do is take your eyes off the vanishing point that you believe to be the end of the corridor, the climax of your plot, and look around you. Notice the windows and doors lining the corridor. Open them.

So, how do we actually apply this metaphor to your immediate experience? When you're done reading this paragraph, look up again. Look around you. Make note of the things that instantly attract your attention. Then ignore those things and study the things that seem completely insignificant or irrelevant. After this initial inventory, choose the most insignificant thing you can find and make it the center of your attention. Focus your gaze upon it and contemplate it. How did it come to be? Why did it come to be? If manmade, who made it, under what possible conditions, and why? How did the world come to manifest itself in this thing in this fashion? Follow the likely path of its components as far back in time and as far outward in space as your knowledge and imagination will allow you, as far back as the Big Bang, if you can.

    This thing has travelled from the very beginning of the universe to be here now, at the center of your attention. The material components of your being too have travelled from the beginning of time and space to be here now, in communion with this thing before you. This is neither metaphor nor melodrama. It is a fundamental physical fact of your existence. Whatever it is on which you sit or lie has risen through time and space, likely with the assistance of hundreds of hands, to hold you up now. Everything around you is "important."

    One belief that is common to nearly all spiritual traditions is the belief that we are here to bear witness to the world, that we are here ultimately to experience existence, to pay attention to it. The extent to which we lock our perceptions onto certain privileged aspects of that existence, like lab rats fixating on a food lever, is the extent to which we fail to bear witness to our lives, the extent to which we cease being the ones actually living our lives. Your attention is your life. Be mindful of what you are giving your life to. Even things that you already enjoy will be enhanced by this mindfulness. If you like coffee, for example, try to give your undivided attention to the next sip. Block everything else out of your consciousness but the taste and aroma of that coffee. Even if it's not the "best" coffee, you will remember it for days... years... a lifetime.

Unsolvable Mysteries

In Western societies, the predominant attitude toward mysteries is that they are meant to be solved and that they can all be solved. Not only does this attitude fuel one of the most popular genres in literature, film, and television, but it's the fuel on which the scientific method runs as well. I too enjoy solving a good mystery, but a great danger lurks within the belief that all mystery can be solved. First of all, it is delusional. Even if we limit our definition of "mystery" to the popular subset of mystery known as "murder mystery," a huge percentage of actual murders are never solved within anyone's lifetime. For example, in America approximately a third are never solved. If we expand the definition of mystery to include anything we don't know or understand, mysteries are never really solved. In fact, every time we learn something new, it raises additional questions, so mystery only multiplies when you try to do away with it.

    The reason I bring up mystery is because the root of the desire to solve mysteries is the same root that feeds our desire to identify ourselves. It is the desire to assign meaning to things, to define them. Until they are interpreted, explained, and defined, they are mysteries. When someone dies, we want to know why. What caused it? If there was a human cause, what was the story behind it? What role did the victim play in the story? What was the motivation of the culprit? To ask such questions is natural, but to assume that answers will be produced forthwith is dangerous, because it can drive us mad if they aren't. The same goes for our own identities. No matter how rigidly we might try to define ourselves, the world will always find ways to challenge and question that definition. If we are unable to be comfortable with uncertainty, if we are unwilling to tolerate ambiguity in our roles and in their relationship to the roles of others, we run the risk of madness. Such rigid identities inevitably shatter. Feeling comfortable with ambiguity and mystery is an important trait to cultivate if you are going to succeed at recalibrating yourself. It is a necessary aspect of the defamiliarization process.

  The easiest and most effective recommendation I can think of for increasing one's tolerance of mystery is to read literature. Read literary fiction, not the kind of popular fiction that is often misleadingly called "genre" or "plot-driven." The common characteristic of popular fiction is that the protagonists always succeed at achieving their goals. There is ultimately no uncertainty or ambiguity about these stories, which perpetuates the myth that all mystery is solvable. You should feed your imagination with stories that don't explain away mystery. Read nonfiction that challenges your assumptions about the world. Read history. Read philosophy. Read biography and autobiography to introduce yourself to different ways others have experienced the world. And most of all, read poetry. Read poetry that you don't quite "get," and don't grasp after the meaning of it. Let it wash over you. Even if you have no idea what's going on, it's working. It's making you more comfortable with ambiguity. But watch out: if you read enough, it might start making sense!

Everyday Eternity

There's a twofold purpose to this exercise. The first is to simulate the expansive feeling of eternity that can push back assumed psychological boundaries. The second is to counteract restrictive biases about the relative significance of your surroundings. What we're going to do is practice taking "mental photographs" of your surroundings. What I mean by this is to let your eyes rest on something around you and imagine that it is frozen in a photograph forever, frozen just as it appears now, the instant you look at it. Study it as if this image is framed and hanging on the wall of an art gallery... forever. Eternity can be terrifying if you are thinking about your self in relation to it, so don't do that. Look entirely outward at this image before you. Forget about yourself. You are the image, persisting in the moment of the image, as a work of art.

You might want to begin this exercise with things you usually consider beautiful, but don't stop there. Do it with scenes that you find completely ordinary. Even the ordinary, removed from time by the imagination, becomes art, becomes extraordinary. Eventually, you will want to do this with things you habitually consider depressing or ugly. Freeze a storm cloud into a mental photograph and savor it as art, rather than seeing it as an irritating, perhaps even fear-inducing, entity. If you feel that you need more practice with actual photography before attempting this exercise, visit an art museum and study the photography there. Practice taking actual photos with your phone, but make sure that these particular photos are of ordinary, unremarkable things, and then study them as though they are blown up and hanging on the wall of that art museum. What do they teach you about time? What do they teach you about the nature of beauty and "meaning"?

As with all of these exercises, it is important not to be self-conscious. Be self-aware, not self-conscious. If you are being self-conscious, you are judging yourself the way you imagine the dominant members of your society would be judging you, were they to be aware of what you were doing. That is precisely the kind of thinking we are trying to undo, to take the power of decision-making from that imagined group and give it back to you. Allow yourself to feel whatever the photographs suggest to you. Let the images wash over you. Let them carry you where they will.

You Are Everywhere

Much of the existential anguish we experience as humans results from the limited scale routinely used to measure time and space in many current cultures. Particularly in the West, the largest unit of time people are habitually used to imagining is the duration of their own personal lifespan, as though time begins when they are conceived and ends when they die. As for space, the personal physical space that most of us associate with our body is not usually larger than that extending a foot or so from our body, with even shorter distances in densely populated areas.

The implication of this for identity formation is that Westerners tend to have a rather limited sense of the scope of their identities in space and time. We tend to feel separated from both our ancestors and our descendants by an insurmountable gulf of time, and we tend to feel equally as separated in physical space from anyone not actually touching us. This enhances the difficulty many feel trying to understand the identities of others and how they interrelate with our own. It is a tremendous, culture-wide failure of the imagination. Fortunately, the human imagination is capable of astounding feats, when harnessed properly. That's where the next two exercises come in.

We'll begin with space. This is a fairly common yoga mediation, so it might feel familiar to some of you. First, sit in a comfortable location, preferably one where you can still hear ambient noise some distance away. Then close your eyes and with your mind "feel" that thin envelope of personal space around you, feel the closeness and comfort of it. Now the heavy lifting begins: with your mind, consciously expand that personal space to include the entire room in which you sit, or the equivalent amount of space if you are outside, allowing everything within that room to feel close and personal to you, as if it is touching you.

Once you have achieved a feeling of intimacy with the entire room, push that space out even further, enveloping the entire neighborhood, taking all those ambient noises (birds singing, cars honking, dogs barking, etc.) into your personal space. Feel that they are all with you… within what you consider to be your space… within you. When you have achieved a feeling of intimacy with this unit of distance, expand it again and again, exponentially expanding the distance each time. Envelope the entire city or county in your personal space, then the state, the nation, the continent, the hemisphere, the Earth. Of course, at one level or another it will become a fairly abstract exercise for you, depending upon the detail of your knowledge of physical and human geography, but it will be a useful exercise for expanding both your emotional imagination and your sense of self.

Next let's work on expanding our sense of personal time, which is very similar to our sense of three-dimensional space, but in the fourth dimension. In this exercise, the personal space immediately around us extends from yesterday to tomorrow. If we extend this analogy, we can think of the current week as being like the room in which we sit, and we can think of the months before and the months to come as being like the sounds of the neighborhood outside, and so on. As you expand the envelope of time that feels close to you, it will become an increasingly abstract exercise, as your memory of the past and your imagination of the future become hazier, but the important thing is that you feel close to those entities, no matter how abstract or emblematic they become. When you reach the beginning and the end of your own life, continue on, following the strands of your personal DNA backward in time through your ancestors, toward its primordial origin, and forward in time through your descendants, toward its final living expression. Make each expanse as personal as the moment you call "now."

In fact, there is a variation of this personal time exercise that some of you might also find useful. Whether inspired by the ancient Greek philosopher Zeno or by Zen or Einstein, we may subdivide the duration of an instant infinitely, meaning that the distinction between a second and a century is negligible from the perspective of eternity. In other words, you are experiencing eternity right now. All of time is fractally encapsulated here. All of time exists right now, expanding outward from the fulcrum of this moment. Your sense of time is relative to your sensory and cultural conditioning. What this means is that you can harness this reality to help you expand your personal sense of time. In a similar fashion to what we did in the "Everyday Eternity" chapter, fix your eyes on something stationary and focus on the moment, feeling all the "space" within it. Feel the moment expanding endlessly. The entirety of time is within this moment, and the moment is entirely within you.

Exposure

Exposure is a psychotherapeutic technique developed to help people overcome phobias by subjecting them to the object of their fear, under professional supervision, until they become desensitized toward that fear. It's usually quite effective but can, naturally, be very unsettling... until it starts working. What I'm going to propose here is a much more pleasant version of exposure that you can practice on your own. Of course, the goal of this exercise will not be to overcome phobias but to overcome prejudices, which, as I touched upon in the "Haunted Mansion" chapter, are usually related to fears.

Keep in mind that we don't need to purge ourselves of all prejudices. Having distinct preferences or tastes can be a source of great pleasure, but when we take our preferences too seriously and begin to either impose them on others or allow them to influence our decisions in ways that alienate or injure others, we need to take a step back and reevaluate those preferences. For example, I'm perfectly entitled to have musical preferences, but if I have such a strong aversion to a certain type of music that it causes me emotional distress to hear it, and if I avoid people whom I associate with that type of music, I've clearly got an issue I need to address, particularly if that music is actually enjoyed by others. Until I can at least achieve a glimmer of appreciation for why others listen to that music, I'm not functioning as a fully aware social being. That's where exposure can come in handy, and it's quite simple too.

All you have to do is take something that you thoroughly dislike, particularly something you associate with an identity group different than any of your identity groups, and combine it in the same experience with something you find pleasurable. For example, if you hate country music and love milk chocolate, eat milk chocolate while listening to country music. If you hate hip-hop and love back-rubs, have someone give you a back-rub while listening to hip-hop. If you hate the color pink and love country music, stare at something pink while listening to country music.

This is a conditioning exercise, which means you will have to repeat it a number of times, so start with small doses of the dislike (short durations, low volumes, etc.) and increase them a little each time you repeat the experience, perhaps with a different pleasure source involved each time. You probably don't want to overdo it with the chocolate. Make sure the amount of pleasure you are experiencing always outweighs the displeasure, so you don't run the risk of tipping the scale in the wrong direction and contaminating your pleasure sources. With alterations to the details, you can apply this exercise to just about any dislike of yours.

Again, the goal isn't to force yourself to love something new. In general, it would be nice if you could increase your capacity for loving different aspects of the world, but that's not likely to happen with something you formerly detested. The goal here is to diminish the unconscious control that your dislikes have over you, by neutralizing them a bit with the antidote of pleasure. That will provide you with more control over prejudices that currently feel almost like instincts. Fortunately, they aren't instincts. If everyone doesn't have them, they've been acquired from our surroundings and are likely the result of social conditioning designed to perpetuate identities that ultimately serve the interests of the ruling classes.

Also, don't worry that an exercise like this is going to somehow erase an identity you currently enjoy. The worst that could happen is that you add a new complement to the vast array of identities you already possess. You would be increasing your capacity for appreciating the world and, consequently, expanding your sense of self.

Stretch!

Make a list of things other people like but that you either dislike or that make you feel uncomfortable:

(Now, one at a time, over the following days, expose yourself to them in the ways described in this last chapter.)

Systematic Derangement of the Senses

The phrase "systematic derangement of the senses" comes to us, via translation, from Arthur Rimbaud, the 19th century enfant terrible of French letters, responsible for some of the most innovative poetry of the period. The phrase originated in a letter in which he explains to a former teacher his beliefs about the proper role of a poet in society, which for him was meant to be a visionary role, one that involved rigorous experimentation and awareness of all possible ways the human experience could manifest itself. For him, as for many, the poet's role was essentially prophetic, a role akin to that of a priest or priestess in pre-Modern societies. In fact, as radical as "systematic derangement of the senses" might sound, it is simply a more intense version of the defamiliarization that we discussed earlier. It has been practiced by humans seeking visionary inspiration as far back as anthropologists feel comfortable making claims about the human experience.

There are many systematic methods by which such a state of consciousness is sought, including but not limited to, drumming and chanting; fasting; sleep deprivation; spinning, like that practiced by Sufi Dervishes; extreme physical exertion; and, of course, at the more intense end of the spectrum, the ritual ingestion of psychoactive substances like mescaline and psilocybin. Though the intensity of experiences resulting from the different methods vary, there are commonalities across the spectrum of approaches. Practitioners often describe a greater feeling of unity with the universe, as if the distinction between self and other dissolves.

In a sense, the experience overwhelms one's habitual understanding of the world, temporarily washing away routine concerns by the intensity of the experience. Even later, after the experience has subsided, one's priorities have been recontextualized within the broader scope provided by the experience. One is less likely, for example, to be perturbed by a comment about one's clothing, if one has recently concluded a week-long fast. Priorities will have been sufficiently reframed so that the comment will seem insignificant... possibly even alien.

Now, I realize that many readers aren't interested in becoming so defamiliarized with their conventional understanding of things that comments about clothing seem alien to them, though I'm also sure some would welcome that. Nor would I recommend a number of the methods mentioned above, at least without professional guidance. However, it would be careless of us to dismiss wholesale all such practices in our endeavor to understand the greater context of our identities and how they might align more harmoniously with the actual, rather than the assumed, reality of our physical and cultural environments.

In fact, I have an extremely common exercise that can systematically alter your senses in a fashion that will provide you with many of the psychological benefits mentioned above: exercise. That is physical exercise itself... pushed to your personal limit. Regardless of how "in shape" you might be, if you are able to safely perform some kind of physical exertion to the point of complete exhaustion, you will find yourself in a state very similar to that of a selfless trance. You aren't going to suddenly be granted enlightenment, but by reminding the body of its mortal limits, lesser concerns diminish in significance, at least briefly, and priorities are reframed within the context of extreme physical exhaustion, which, though it is probably far away, assuming you don't have a heart condition, always feels closely related to physical extinction.

    The next time you completely exhaust yourself, lie down wherever it is permissible to do so and allow your eyes to gaze upward without intent to grasp anything. Allow every facet of your mind to unfocus. Don't "think" about anything. Feel your lungs feast on the atmosphere, the burn of your muscles subsiding to a succulent warmth, the throb of blood coursing through your body, the delicious lassitude of your nerve endings seeming to melt into the world around you, even the wavering and warping of your visual field, as your eyes relax and unfocus. In this state, everything will feel far away for at least a moment, and, when you come back to your self, you will feel as though you have been away on a refreshing journey to the actual world that is.

The Intelligence of Fire

For over a million years, humans have been staring into campfires. These fires have kept us warm, kept us safe from predators, and cooked the food that allowed us to develop our current physiology. Fire and language are two of our oldest tools, ones that have cooperatively influenced our evolution. This is one of the reasons why fire is so mesmerizing to the human mind. When we look into a fire, we are seeing what our ancestors saw all the way back to the beginning of the human race. We feel what they felt.

    I'm not being poetic here. When our senses take in a tame fire, the sight and sound and smell and feel of it, we are placed back into our original, Paleolithic mind, like a baby back in its cradle. The feeling we experience is what made us capable of harnessing one of nature's most destructive forces: we are profoundly at ease in its presence. If our ancestors weren't at ease with it, we wouldn't be here. We would have been just another extinct hominid species. It could be claimed that fire is the mother of modern humanity… which could go far in explaining the behavior of this particular child.

    I won't attempt an identity detox of the entire species, but I will postulate that one of the reasons electronic screens, such as televisions and smart phones, are so mesmerizing to children is because they stimulate the child's ancestral memory of fire. The child feels as though she is in the presence of a benevolent, flickering guardian spirit... though, of course, she is not. The device is simply hijacking the child's inborn fascination with fire. I say "child" only because it is particularly difficult for children to control this impulse, though, of course, most adults feel the powerful pull as well, which partially explains both the success of television and the prevalence of pyromania across cultures.

The exercise I am now going to recommend is the simplest exercise in this book. All you have to do is build a fire and stare at it! Of course, make sure your fire is tame, meaning it is safe and contained. It should preferably be surrounded by darkness. A campfire at night simulates our Paleolithic past best. When you stare at it, make sure you are silent, and try to clear your mind of all thought. Let your mind consume the flames. Let the light and warmth and odor of it wash over your senses. Listen to the crackle of it. Your goal is to sink into that recess where your ancestors sleep. Don't worry, you won't turn into a cave man, but in that state of fire-consciousness, your identity will be ever-so-slightly realigned to be closer to the fundamental identity of humanity that we all unconsciously share. We are all there still, sitting around the fire at the heart of our great human encampment.

Being Water

There are limits to the number of ways that human nature can assume identity, based on fundamental physical and sensory limitations, but the number of identities possible is still vast. Water can be used as an effective metaphor for understanding the nature of human identity. There are certain fundamental physical limitations to the chemical composition of water, in order for it to be called water, just as there are limitations to what can be called Homo sapiens, but water can yet assume a plethora of forms that we experience as unique identities, depending on the conditions of the environment in which it is found, even down to the mineral and microbial content of it at the microscopic level.

  For this exercise, which is designed to impress upon us the fluid nature of identity, we start by picturing a relatively small quantity of water, perhaps the amount contained within your physical body… or less. Then we imaginatively follow that body of water on a great cycle around the world, across the expanses of time that it takes for it to do so, making note of the different characters or identities that this water-self assumes on its journey: clouds, snow, rain, mountain streams, water falls, marshes, swamps, lakes, seas, subterranean rivers, icebergs, oceans, cold salt rivers beneath those oceans, tsunamis, monsoons… Try to imagine yourself embarking on this journey. How does your perception of yourself change with each new environment? What body of water do you feel most "like" at this point in your life? What bodies of water do you think others identify with most? Did you feel like them when you imagined yourself passing through that same body?

Being Wild

In Western societies, our identities as humans are ultimately defined by what is considered to be nonhuman, for "human" is often considered the foundational identity upon which all other identities are built. Integrally linked to the distinction between human and nonhuman is the distinction between "civilized" and "wild." These are completely arbitrary distinctions that betray a Western prejudice regarding the relationship between humans and their environment, the assumption that a "natural" environment is inherently nonhuman until it is humanized. Thus the historic role of Western humans has been to tame or civilize the wilderness.

In reality, humans do not inhabit some rarified state of existence outside of nature. Everything that exists is nature, including humans. Just as a wildebeest is no less "evolved" than a human, neither is a wildebeest any more wild than a human. Believing we are less wild than other natural entities is not only thoroughly unscientific, but it also ultimately leads to destructive behavior, the kind of behavior that results from believing one is not part of one's environment. When one believes he is breathing different air than those around him, that air will eventually run out.

So, how do we counteract this dangerous identity formation? Well, simply acknowledging it is a good start, but we can also practice placing ourselves in environments that we have come to consider "wild," and to practice a version of radical empathy there. You don't need to travel to Yosemite. Any place where you feel that you are somewhat "out of place" will work. Depending on the extent of your cultural programming, you might even feel that by simply sitting in a park you represent a small human intrusion into the "wild." If so, sit there and remind yourself that you are part of nature.

    Perhaps you choose to sit in a forest or a swamp. Do the same thing. If you are respectful of the place, you have the right to form a personal connection with it. Repeat the mental mantra "I belong here, on this Earth." Don't worry about what you would eat or how you would clothe yourself. Humans have adapted to every environment on Earth. You could do it if you really wanted to. The goal of this exercise is simply to remind yourself that you are not excluded from this place. You are as welcomed here as you are in a high-rise office building. In fact, it's very possible that you are more welcome in a swamp than in a high-rise, depending on which swamp and which high-rise. Just sit quietly and pay attention to what's happening around you and remind yourself that you are a meaningful part of it.

Re-setting Yourself

As I mentioned before, identity is formed predominantly through the childhood process by which individuals adapt to their social surroundings, a process analogous to first-language acquisition. Our childhood environment is the context within which our identity is formed. It was the air we breathed, and, because we absorbed the culture unconsciously, it tends to remain as invisible to us as the air we are literally breathing right now. This is why it is difficult for many people to understand the identities of "others," because they didn't grow up in the same environments and therefore have trouble imagining all the nuances of having done so. This also explains the great appeal of travel for some people. Experiencing "foreign" cultures is one of the most common ways people come to recognize the uniqueness, and often arbitrariness, of their own native cultures. For many, the experience can even result in something like an identity detox. Fortunately, however, the expenses of international travel are not necessary to produce such a result.

  I have adapted an exercise from one sometimes employed in playwriting workshops. The playwriting version is used to generate tension and provide motivation for characters. The premise is fairly simple on the outset: remove a character from their usual environment and place them in one where they feel "out of their element." Then let the dialogue begin. For example, the playwright might have a banker stumble into a blue-color bar or a priest waiting at the corner for a bus finds himself unexpectedly in the company of sex workers. The possibilities for this type of exercise are endless, even within the borders of a single city.

Our exercise will not be for the purpose of creating compelling drama but to help us understand how dependent our identities are upon our habitual surroundings and how awkward it can be for people with "other" identities to navigate them, outside of their own familiar environments. We are going to take ourselves out of context. For this thought experiment, you should select an identity group that is often considered to be in opposition to one of the identity groups with which you are associated. Now imagine that you are alone with a number of people from that oppositional identity group, in an environment where they would feel comfortable. Take note of how you feel. Consider how you would interact with them and how they would interact with you.

Now, for the second and more challenging part of the exercise, in your imagination transport a member of that opposition group to an environment in which you are comfortable and contemplate how that person would likely feel in this environment. How would they likely behave? How would they interact with others in this environment? How would they likely be treated?

Finally, imagine both of you are together in an environment that is foreign to you both, perhaps even an environment that feels hostile. How will both of you likely feel now? How will you behave toward one another? Know that anyone you consider to be an enemy could become a friend with nothing more than a change of setting.

Stretch!

Seek out a public place that you wouldn't normally frequent. Sit down with this book and observe the environment and social atmosphere around you. Make note here of anything that catches your attention, for later reflection:

Radical Empathy

From his letters, it is clear that the poet John Keats thought one of the most important responsibilities of a poet was to cultivate the ability to transcend the limitations of one's identity and experience the world from the perspectives of others, including even nonhuman and inanimate entities, in order to better understand existence itself. In fact, he went so far as to claim that poets have no identity or self, though I believe this was more of an aspirational claim, one that helped him feel liberated from some of the more burdensome identities imposed upon him by circumstances beyond his control, such as poverty and tuberculosis. Of course, we do not all want to be poets, but by now we should be able to recognize the importance of Keats' goal in one's effort to recognize and remove unwanted, inherited prejudice from one's own identities.

Practicing what I am calling "radical empathy," Keats would completely give over his mind to imagining what it would feel like to be someone or something else, whether it was another person in a crowded room, a sparrow pecking at the gravel beneath his window, or a billiard ball rolling across the felted slate of a pool table.

For our immediate purpose, we don't need to imagine the lives of sparrows or billiard balls, though I do encourage you to give it a try some time. For now, let us imagine the daily life and emotions of someone other than yourself. Try to fill yourself with what you imagine they would be feeling at this very moment in their day. If this exercise is initially difficult for you, choose someone close to you, someone whom you feel you understand fairly well already... but preferably someone who you know thinks differently about a few issues that are important to you. This will help "stretch" your emotional imagination, what you are able to allow yourself to feel. Don't worry, your imagination won't suddenly snap or be stretched out of shape or "turn to the dark side." It will simply become more flexible, and you, consequently, will gain greater control over it.

Once you have tried this exercise on a few subjects who are close to you, and you feel that you can handle more weight, select a subject who you feel is more distant from you in overall sentiment. Eventually, if you are going to take this exercise as far as you can, you will want to choose a subject whom you hate, without judging the emotions you imagine that person is feeling. Again, this isn't going to turn you into an emotional jellyfish. On the contrary, it will make it less likely that you will be shocked by unexpected encounters with others. You will be more capable of remaining calm under emotional duress because you will have already been in a similar place, under the controlled conditions of this exercise.

Memento Mori

The last stretching exercise I will suggest was actually a common practice in the West up until modern times. "Memento Mori" is a Latin phrase that means essentially "Remember you die," and memento mori meditations often consisted of contemplations of symbols of death, such as death masks or paintings of human skulls.

The point of such contemplations wasn't morbid curiosity but to bring to mind the inevitability of one's own mortality and to thus provide one with a more expansive perspective on life, diminishing the seeming significance of daily preoccupations that can weigh heavily on our minds despite their ultimate lack of substance on the scales of life and death. When you fully acknowledge, for example, that your skeleton, the only part of your physical being that will remain a hundred years from now, is always here with you, just beneath your skin, your neighbor's opinion of the length of your grass suddenly seems extremely insignificant, because it is, just as your opinion of your neighbor's lawn is equally insignificant when considered beside the inevitability of your departure from this life. This contemplation corrects priorities and exposes biases like no other.

- *I am going to die. I should spend more time with loved ones.*

- *I am going to die. I should recognize the miracle of a bird singing in a tree.*
- *I am going to die. I should be kind to my neighbor while we are both still alive.*

Part III: Practice

The Snow Man

One must have a mind of winter
To regard the frost and the boughs
Of the pine-trees crusted with snow;

And have been cold a long time
To behold the junipers shagged with ice,
The spruces rough in the distant glitter

Of the January sun; and not to think
Of any misery in the sound of the wind,
In the sound of a few leaves,

Which is the sound of the land
Full of the same wind
That is blowing in the same bare place

For the listener, who listens in the snow,
And, nothing himself, beholds
Nothing that is not there and the nothing that is.

Wallace Stevens

You should now be ready to engage in the more complex exercises that constitute the final stage of our workout. The following chapters will take your newly enhanced self-awareness to the next level, preparing you for the implementation of that awareness in your interactions with others. Now that you have strengthened and stretched your understanding of self and identity, it is time to begin practicing the skills and drills that will make you a nimbler actor on the field of human action.

Let us begin by reading "The Snow Man" together. Wallace Stevens understood the human imagination perhaps better than anyone else living in the 20th century, and yet, here he provides us with a seemingly counter-intuitive lesson, coming from a champion of the imagination. He recommends that, if we want to understand winter, we must stand in it for so long that the cold no longer bothers us, so long we no longer hear misery in the wind. When all our preconceptions have dropped away and we have returned to the open state of our original self, when our identities have dropped away and we have become "nothing" ourselves, we will finally see "Nothing that is not there." We will no longer see what we imagine to be there or what we've been told is there. We will see only what is actually there.

In characteristic Stevens' fashion, he leaves us with one final paradox to contemplate, to remind us of the importance of mystery. In the final phrase of the poem, he claims that in this state of complete openness we will also be able to see the nothing that IS there, a nothing which I personally take to mean the infinite that is always present within the finite... However, the interpretation of this final, enigmatic statement is ultimately left to each individual reader to contemplate for their self.

    Don't worry, none of the following exercises will ask us to stand in the cold until we are enlightened, but they will be asking us to engage in similarly challenging mental exercises that can lead to realizations nearly as profound as that of Stevens' snow man, realizations that can provide us tremendously practical assistance in our interpersonal relations.

Negative Capability

In a letter to his brothers, written in December of 1817, John Keats described what he considered to be the premier trait of a person of "achievement." He called it "negative capability," and when his letters were later published, the concept was embraced, and the wisdom of it revered, by poets worldwide. The definition Keats provides in the letter is brief but incisive: "When man is capable of being in uncertainties, Mysteries, doubts, without any irritable reaching after fact and reason." Though Keats used Shakespeare as the model of one who was negatively capable, he considered it a practice common to those of great accomplishment in any field, and, though it has been consciously cultivated primarily by poets since then, its application is still as relevant as ever to anyone who desires to check their own limits.

By "negative" he did not imply the pessimism or cynicism that is commonly associated with the term now, but rather the word's invocation of absence, the absence or lack of definition, even the opposite of what has been given shape in mind or space. One who is negatively capable is able to simultaneously harbor both a belief and its opposite or the absence of that belief, without feeling a debilitating sense of contradiction or paradox. Instead, this state of suspended judgement is experienced by the practitioner as the truest state of being. In this state, one inhabits a realm of infinite potential, infinite possibility.

One can believe that what one has been taught is possibly as true as its mirror negative. For example, a 16th century practitioner might have allowed herself to believe the Earth is the center of a thoroughly understood universe while also allowing herself to seriously entertain the notion that the Earth inhabits the remote periphery of a virtually unknown universe. One could believe that punishment for a social transgression is an ethical necessity as well as an act of inhumanity. In a particularly profound state of negative capability, one could believe that the choice to be or not to be is ultimately arbitrary. In order to act, of course, one must eventually snap out of it and make a decision, but the cultivation and practice of negative capability presents one with new choices, new solutions, and a perspective that is both broader and more nuanced than before.

The simplest way to practice negative capability is to select a firmly held belief of yours and conduct a thought experiment by which you imagine that you believe the opposite of that concept, explaining to yourself ways in which it could possibly be true. The point isn't to change your mind but to expand it. Again, don't worry that you will suddenly change your fundamental beliefs and become someone else. This is, in fact, the purpose of the exercise: to erase the fear that if you listen to others you will become them. You will not, but you will be able to hear them better, because you will have a more sophisticated understanding of your own beliefs and their relation to those of others. You will be less likely to be blinded by fear of the "other," fear of the perceived opposite of yourself. You will have inhabited that place in your own mind, even if you settle back to your own habitual beliefs afterward.

I'll illustrate how one might conduct such a thought experiment, using an example I touched upon earlier. Having been raised by atheists, my usual assumption about the human place in the universe is that we came to be as a result of chemical reactions made possible by the evolving environmental conditions on one planet among countless others, no one of them more unique than any of the rest. However, if I am to practice negative capability, I must convince myself, at least for the duration of the experiment, that this planet, these people, and, ultimately, this self all occupy a special place in some grand scheme, that they occupy a central position in the universe. "How could this be possible," I begin by asking myself.

Perhaps, I might speculate, the universe is indeed like a giant expanding sphere, as many physicists maintain, with the surface of that sphere consisting of all the matter, space, and time of which the universe is composed. Inside and outside the sphere are outside space and time, beyond what we currently know. The surface is everything we can now know. It feels like maybe I'm onto something, so I explore that idea more. Where, I ask myself, is the center of the surface of this sphere? When I consider this, I feel a curious tug in my gut, a tingling sensation ripple through my limbs.

Something is about to hit me. I know because I've felt it before, every time I've created a good work of art.

Where is the middle of the skin of a sphere? You can place a dot anywhere on the surface of a ball and consider it the center of the surface that expands away from it in every direction. Any point on the surface of the ball can equally be considered the center of the surface of the ball. You can place your finger anywhere on that ball and spin it on the tip of your finger. Therefore, if the universe is anything like the model physicists use to explain the universe, every infinitely divisible point in the universe is the center of the universe. The tip of your nose, as you read this now, is the center of the universe. If you raise your eyes from the page, whatever your gaze falls upon is the center of the universe. Your eye is the center. Whatever you are thinking just now, however sacred or profane: the center of the universe.

So, what do I do with this new idea I've uncovered? Does it completely replace my old learned belief that human existence is irredeemably dwarfed in significance by the cold, impersonal vastness of space? It's unlikely that I will ever completely replace that old belief, but I now allow both ideas to coexist without any "irritable reaching after fact" to steady me, without willful ignorance of anything that contradicts one belief or the other. I now have a more sophisticated appreciation for the subject than I did before.

Allow yourself to be "multitudes," as Walt Whitman advised by example, and luxuriate in the simultaneous definition and expansion of self that results. Take one belief at a time and apply negative capability to it. Turn it inside out. Even if you fail in the attempt, you will be healthier for having tried.

Practice!

Think of an argument you have had or witnessed recently and outline the main points of a persuasive case for both sides of the argument (also think of other sides that there could be to the argument):

Mental Hierarchies

We each have a complex, three-dimensional model of the world imbedded in our mind. This model is similar to the maps I described earlier, but its main feature is the interconnected vertical categories of value that it contains. In many societies, the orientation of each of these category-hierarchies places the most valuable or desirable entity at the "top" (skyward) and the least valuable or desirable entity at the "bottom" (earthward), resulting in spectrums of value that suggest to us how important any particular entity is, based on where it is located in its corresponding hierarchy in the model.

We rarely ever articulate the details of this model to ourselves, as most of it was unconsciously implanted in childhood by the adults around us, but it nevertheless influences our behavior and our goals. In fact, we tend to judge how "real" something is in the actual world by how much it resembles the details of this imaginary model. This, in part, accounts for the notorious fallibility of human memory, since we can only remember what we are capable of imagining. If we can't imagine something to be true, it simply can't be true, even if we're staring right at it.

We consciously access these models nearly every time we go shopping, comparing the perceived quality of products with their relative costs, often compromising between the two. It can be quite a complex mental calculus, but we are used to it in consumer capitalist societies. However, outside of human resource offices, most of us are not used to consciously making these calculations in regard to other humans. The calculations happen, nevertheless. For most of us, they simply happen under the radar of our conscious awareness, when we instinctively compare our perceived reality with the predetermined model of reality in our imaginations, and we make a nearly instantaneous decision based on where we perceive someone else to be in that model hierarchy and which decision the model suggests we should make in order to defend or improve our position in that hierarchy. Perhaps we cross the street to avoid passing someone on the sidewalk. Perhaps we reach for our phone in anticipation of calling the police. Perhaps we overlook someone in favor of someone else for a promotion.

We have hierarchies for all kinds of identities, including even nonhuman identities. For a quick illustration, let's consider the way most people talk about evolution. As any evolutionary biologist could tell us, there is not a single species on Earth that is "more evolved" than any other species. They have all taken the same amount of time to arrive at their current forms, evolving nonstop the entire time. They are all equally well adapted to the niche they have been inhabiting in their part of the ecosystem. To say that a human is more evolved than a butterfly is nonsensical. Can we do what butterflies do? Not in a million years. Possibly in a hundred million… but I digress. My point is that the hierarchical way we often think about evolution is completely imaginary, with no actual relation to reality, and the same is true of the hierarchical ways we think about human identity.

Let's consider professions, for an example. If you ask a random person on the street what role they consider to be more "important," that of a trash collector or a medical doctor, your answer is most likely going to be the doctor. If you pressed them further for rationale, likely reasons would be the amount of education the doctor underwent, the likelihood of the doctor being able to save someone's life, or, begging the question, the relative size of the doctor's salary. Such rationale betrays a significant amount of social conditioning, in addition to making significant assumptions about individuals actually performing these roles. A trash collector, for example, might very well have a PhD in Philosophy and, hopefully, would be responsible for far fewer deaths than, say, a physician who could easily be guilty of overprescribing painkillers.

The "education" rationale for the choice of the doctor being more "important" would likely seem to be the most sensible rationale to most people, but it really isn't "education" that is being valued here, for even if you were to inform your interviewee that, in his spare time, the trash collector has been educating himself rigorously about the history, philosophy, and science of trash collection, and has been doing so for decades, your interviewee would still likely say the physician is more important. Why?

If you continued your questioning, perhaps your interviewee would then retreat to the second rationale, that they would rather have the physician around if they were to become deathly ill, ignoring, of course, that this is far less statistically likely than that they will need their trash collected every week, for as long as they live in the city and abide by residential ordinances... that, in fact, they are far more likely to become deathly ill by contagion or pollution if such collection ceases or is conducted improperly.

If we can agree that both professions are equally necessary for society to continue functioning more-or-less the way it is currently, then why, exactly, is one profession higher on the model hierarchy of this society? Do physicians work harder than trash collectors? Are they more intelligent? Are they more "evolved"? Hopefully these questions sound ridiculous to you, as they are meant to be. The most likely actual reason for the physician's position being higher in the hierarchy is that, yes, the education process is difficult, but anyone who's willing to put in the time and effort can do it... and, if they go to school in America, they can then graduate and suffer the privilege of a crushing personal debt that necessitates a relatively higher salary to pay off. That's why they're valued more than trash collectors. Should they be? Of course not. Perhaps they should be pitied more often than they are currently, but not valued more than trash collectors. It's only a combination of unconsciously learned prejudices that make them so for most people. Remember, the purpose of this example hasn't been to value physicians less, but to value trash collectors more, to understand the ultimately arbitrary nature of our learned prejudices when it comes to hierarchies of identity.

The exercise with which I will end this chapter is simple but can be incredibly effective at recalibrating your assumptions. Essentially, what you do is what I just did above with my physician/trash collector example. First, select an identity category. I chose professions for my example, but feel free to select any type of category. If you're having trouble thinking of a category that you want to use, refer to the list of identity types mentioned in "The Mansion of Yourself" chapter for some ideas. Next, select an identity that you consider to be quite high in the hierarchy of that category and one that you consider to be fairly low on that hierarchy, and then deconstruct the assumptions and prejudices that lead you to feel that way.

Finally, find ways to appreciate the identity that is lower on the hierarchy, realistically raising it until it is equal in value with the other identity. If this is challenging for you, take a step back and try something along the lines of the evolution example I used earlier. Explain to yourself how a mosquito is as equally evolved to succeed in its lifestyle as a human is. The point here is to become aware of your mental models of the world and to then appraise the accuracy and ultimate implications of those models. If you are perfectly honest with yourself, you will make some astounding discoveries.

Incidentally, your own personal constellation of identities with which you associate yourself is arranged in a giant metaphoric stack in your unconscious, with the most valued role perched at the top and the rest descending from there in the order in which you invest them with significance, leaving the very bottom position available for your most detested or disregarded role. Through constant unconscious referencing, your daily decision-making reinforces this hierarchy by privileging the options that serve to increase the stability of that hierarchy, eventually resulting in a sum of lifetime decisions that defines who you were and how you fit into the ongoing puzzle of history. If you are ever uncertain about the actual relative value you unconsciously place on different identities of yours, pay close attention to the seemingly instinctive decisions you make, and ask yourself which identities they are actually serving.

Practice!

Make a list of as many of your assigned or chosen identities that you can think of, in order of their value to you. Is your order the same order in which mainstream society would list them?

Mind Over Metaphor

The way we ascribe meaning to the world is primarily accomplished through interlocking systems of metaphor that we unconsciously internalized during our childhood language acquisition process. When we learn languages in adulthood, the inherent logic of those languages is more apparent to us, because we are acquiring them through conscious effort, but our native tongue slips unseen into our mouths and our minds, along with all the prejudices inherent to the logic of that tongue. Now, by "metaphor," I don't mean exclusively the flashy figurative language of poetry that draws attention to itself for the novel way it connects two previously unassociated things, though that is a form of metaphor. I mean any language construction that is not literally true, often associating two entities that are not inherently associated with one another. This includes associations that are made explicitly, such as with simile, metonymy, and what's traditionally called metaphor: for example, "love is like a rose" or "the White House announced today" or "you are such a pig."

    Love and roses are not inherently connected in any way beyond the fact that, according to tradition, in some cultures one might signify their affection for another by giving them a rose; The White House can't literally speak, but it is assumed that the US president lives and works there, so the two are traditionally associated through this common metonymy; and the person being spoken to in the last example is probably not literally a pig, but seems to share some character traits with a pig, such as perhaps slovenly demeanor. Most people easily recognize these as types of metaphor, because the wording is linguistically playful and draws attention to itself.

There are, however, forms of metaphor that are not nearly as noticeable, since they merely imply associations. Nevertheless, they are just as effective at conveying meaning and attitudes, to a great extent because they operate unconsciously, also because they are far more bountiful in any given language than the explicit metaphors of that language. They are also connected with other implied metaphors, creating vast networks of ingrained attitude and meaning within the culture. For example, when you say you're "feeling down," it doesn't mean that you are literally feeling like you are lying on the ground. This is a metaphoric statement that associates the downward direction with depression. In fact, the word "depression" itself is a metaphor associating downward physical pressure with sadness, two experiences that are not necessarily connected, unless you're being crushed to death.

But how do these implicit metaphors convey meaning and influence behavior? To illustrate, I will continue the previous example of "feeling down." Throughout the English language, the downward direction has very consistent associations attached to it. In addition to sadness, and emotion in general, it is associated with physicality, the earth, and with practicality ("down to earth," "down to business," etc.). It is also associated with the extremes of practicality: crassness and baseness, with "earthiness" ("down and dirty"), and even moral ambiguity and deviousness ("that was low"). Ideas and intellect and all things generally considered morally "good" or happy are conventionally linked to the upward direction in English. "Up" is the direction toward which people are expected to aspire, climbing up metaphoric ladders of all kinds.

    Even as a society our most common imaginary goal seems to be space, even though space technically isn't any more "up" than any other direction, since we are "in" space. Priority tends to be given to everything considered "up," which has not been good for the Earth ("down") throughout most of Western history. It also has not been good for groups of people commonly associated with the Earth, like women, who, for example, throughout most of Western history, including right now, are conventionally more closely associated with "Mother Earth" than with "Father Sky." This is not an innocent association. All the characteristics historically associated with downwardness have been stereotypically associated with women (emotional, physical, immoral, etc.), while men have been stereotypically associated with characteristics typically associated with upwardness (intellectual, spiritual, moral, etc.). Fortunately, through the hard work of feminists, society is gaining greater understanding of this particular linguistically ingrained prejudice toward both women and the environment.

    There are many such reinforcing networks of metaphoric prejudice present in any given language. Consider, for example, how you feel about lightness and darkness. Which is usually considered good and which bad in your culture? Is innocence more commonly associated with the color white or with the color black? Have you been culturally trained to associate the color black with "intellectual, spiritual, and moral" or with "emotional, physical, and immoral"? What about the color red? What about the color white? Consider those hierarchies I talked about in the last chapter. What assumptions have you been trained to make based on one's relative upward or downward location in one of those hierarchies? Who would you assume is more "intellectual," a physician or a trash collector? Though both walk the same ground, who is closer to earth and who closer to heaven in your imagination?

    When we start to consciously connect these associated webs of metaphor, it becomes almost terrifying to see how vast is the net that has been cast over us by culture. Do we really have any chance of escaping from prejudices that have been woven so thoroughly into the very fabric of our thought? Of course! We've been working on that throughout this whole book so far. This is just the latest tool in your detox kit: 1) pay attention to metaphor, especially implicit metaphor; 2) question metaphor—for example, one might ask, "why is this 'a dark chapter for America'? Couldn't it just as easily be considered a 'blindingly white chapter'?"; and 3) think of new metaphors, employ less common alternatives to mainstream metaphors, or invert existing metaphoric associations to address unhealthy attitudes—for example, sometimes can it be "Mother Sky" and "Father Earth"?

If you initially have trouble working your way through these steps, poetry can help out. Reading poetry and paying attention to how poets explicitly interrogate, invent, reframe, and extend metaphor will help you do the same with the implicit metaphors that are invisibly guiding your interpretation of the world. Without such effort, your thoughts will struggle to swim free of the strong current of your language.

Practice!

Finish the following statement with as many different metaphoric endings as you can imagine. Try to surprise yourself and challenge conventional thinking:

Love is a...

Defining Yourself

At the cellular level of any culture are the definitions assigned to the world by that culture's language. It is of these definitions that the stories are constructed by which members of that culture live their lives. It is of crucial importance to remember that these definitions are human constructs, adapted to the social and physical environment surrounding the members of any given culture. This means that any definition is subject to reassessment and redefinition, as environments change and as individuals within those cultures consciously choose to revisit existing definitions. That's where this next pair of exercises begins.

    Some of the concepts that are the strongest motivating factors for members of a culture are actually defined quite vaguely in the minds of those individuals. They are equivalent to received assumptions in most people's minds. For example, what is the definition of "success" in your culture? What is your personal definition of "success"? Try to be as detailed as possible with your definition. If you've never defined it for yourself before, why haven't you? If you have defined it, has it changed at all over the years? Subject other important ideas to this same personal definition process. What exactly does "love" mean to you? What about "progress"? "Bravery"? "Freedom"? "Peace"? Etc. How do others define them? Do you agree with them? The sum of such definitions is the animating spirit of the primary identity you inhabit. If you have never examined these abstractions and decided for yourself specifically how you want to define them, you have been following social cues rather than leading a life of your own. Fortunately, it's never too late to start! Take one of the concepts mentioned above and give it a shot.

We'll end this chapter with another related exercise. This one will be familiar to those who have practiced Zen meditation. It is simultaneously the easiest and most difficult exercise one can practice. In fact, don't get frustrated if you have trouble doing it. It's the effort that matters. Here's the exercise: 1) don't think about anything 2) for as long as you can.

The point is to empty your mind, in one sense to start over again, and in another sense to experience the vast, undefined eternity that is always present with you. The longer you are able to do this, the more you are able to reset your existing assumptions and definitions. When you return from nothingness to the world, you will notice things you haven't noticed before. But don't even think about nothingness, for calling something "nothing" defines it, making it something, just like an artificially produced vacuum, which is defined by the shape of the bell jar in which it is being produced. Sustained long enough, it can clear your head for new ways of thinking, feeling, and being. It is one of the surest ways to achieve defamiliarization and subsequent redefinition, simplification, and innovation.

Discomfort Zones

Thought experiments are an important practice for those seeking greater self-awareness, but it is also necessary at times to move beyond the realm of pure thought into its physical embodiment in action. Without this additional step, we are likely to remain within our "comfort zones," and little progress can be made as either individuals or as a society if we restrict ourselves to the environments and relationships with which we are familiar.

Most of us unconsciously seek to recreate the conditions of our childhoods, whether those childhoods were happy or not, because those conditions feel most "normal" to us, regardless of our subsequent age. Conditions other than those in which we were raised tend to feel foreign. They are the way other people live. If our parents fought a lot, as did mine, we tend to have a high tolerance for conflict. We might not even recognize that certain habitual behaviors of ours could be considered intimidating or aggressive by people who don't have as high a threshold for conflict, because their childhoods weren't filled with it.

Without self-awareness, we would tend to gravitate toward others who had similar upbringings, and we would be more likely to start new families with them, families full of the invigorating, heartbreaking violence of our youth. We would be back home again, back where we understood the rules, where we feel normal again, comfortable even. That culture would have successfully used us to replicate itself, thanks to our human emotions, our lack of self-awareness, and because we probably never fully stepped outside our comfort zone to explore a world of nearly infinite alternatives.

Fortunately, we are human, so it's not difficult for us to consciously make ourselves step outside those comfort zones. It begins with something like the thought experiment I described in the "Negative Capability" chapter. Select a firmly held belief or, particularly in this case, a habitual behavior of yours that you've never questioned before and identify what you would consider to be the opposite of that behavior. Then make yourself engage in this opposite behavior, which you consider "not you."

If you consider yourself an introvert, because you feel most comfortable being alone, reach out to someone who seems interesting to you and ask them questions, as an attentive student would, to expand your experience and understanding of other ways of being. You can refer to the instructions in the "Talking to Others" chapter, if you find conversation itself to be an intimidating challenge.

If certain "types" of people make you uneasy, reach out to one and do the same—learn from them. You can always go back to your old ways of thinking, but for the moment you are practicing greatness, literally expanding or greatening yourself. If you find it difficult to do so, assure yourself that you can retreat to within your comfortable boundaries later.

It can be something as simple as going for a long walk around the neighborhood, if you don't consider yourself a physically active person... or because you are intimidated by the neighborhood in which you now find yourself. If you don't like rain, go stand in the rain, with no other purpose than to be in it. Stand there, like Wallace Stevens' snow man, until you are over the misery of it.

I guarantee that you will not have an epiphany every time you do so, but you will be surprised by something that happens or by your reaction to it, surprised in a way that will break the mold of your expectations of reality. A small crack will appear in the rigid structure of your assumptions, and with continued practice you will eventually be able to catch glimpses of a clearer view of reality through that widening crack.

This is why it is often said that "opposites attract." Truth exerts a powerful gravity on the world of human affairs, bending our minds toward it, but rarely from the same direction, and the force seems most compelling when it draws inward from opposite ends of the same axis. The trick is to find the center without violently colliding with those falling from the opposite direction, so you can explore the center together. Making strategic and gradually greater forays beyond your comfort zone, with full knowledge of what you are doing, makes it far more likely that you will be able to locate truth without exploding on impact.

Covers

Most of us are quite familiar with the concept of cover songs and cover bands, but we don't usually give much thought to the critical cultural work they perform. Perhaps the musicians themselves aren't even consciously aware of the significance of their work, because, as an entire society, we haven't given much thought to it. In the West, we are trained to give far more attention to "originality," and our legal system reinforces that prejudice, but without the attitude manifested by a cover, what little understanding our society has of the contingency of identity might be entirely snuffed out.

    Only in theater and music do we commonly witness the phenomenon by which someone takes the work of another and recasts it in a new voice, new body, new role, new style. By appreciating covers, our understanding of the changeable essence of a thing is enhanced. We become aware of the possibility of change in all identities, the inherent contingency and mutability of who we "are." For example, when I hear Lana Del Rey cover "Doin' Time," I suddenly discover a secret door in a room I thought I knew well. Anything could be behind the door: the ocean, the girlfriend mentioned in the song, the community, an even greater sadness and disillusionment than I thought was there before. I start to think differently about Sublime and even about Gershwin, the South, parents and children and love... The lyrics and the melody that form the fundamental self of the song remain, but the song suddenly has a new identity.

This healthy and necessary attitude toward mutability is also understood by translators and interpreters. Transposing the essence of a thing into another medium, such as another language, in this case, is a daily transaction for them. However, the nature of their work is not visible to your average person. Unless you compare different translations of the same text or study the original in its source language, you will not notice the possible variations, the many different ways the identity of the text could have manifested in the new language. This is, of course, far more challenging than listening to a good cover song, but it is perhaps even more effective, if you have the time and inclination to do so.

In addition to exposing yourself to more cover songs, different theatrical productions of the same plays, and ideally different translations of the same literary texts, I recommend that you practice creating covers of your own, to give you a more intimate understanding of the process of transforming identities. The key is to pick something you love (a song, a painting, a poem, a type of food, etc.) and create a new version of it, modifying aspects so that it feels new but is still identifiable as a variation of the original. Not only is this fun, but it will give you intimate insight into the reasons why you like the original, and it will help expand your understanding of identity in general.

Once again, don't be self-conscious when doing this exercise. First of all, no one else needs to know what you're up to. Second, the purpose of this exercise isn't to create works of art. Just think of it as play. Allow yourself to be a child again, defamiliarizing a small piece of a world that has begun to feel all too predictable sometimes. It can be as simple as whistling a song you love, to keep you company in its creation.

Making Mantras

Every culture has mantras it provides to its participants, from the religious chants and prayers we most commonly associate with the term "mantra" to less obvious but equally powerful mantras such as national anthems or marketing slogans. Mantras are incredibly effective ways to reign in one's awareness and focus one's attention on particular aspects of experience. They are usually employed to perpetuate the existence of the culture out of which they emerge, but they can be equally as effective at achieving personal goals, as long as you choose one that you find emotionally resonant.

The way we can employ a personal mantra to assist us in identity detoxification is to create one that you can repeat whenever you feel yourself begin to make assumptions about someone based on what you perceive to be their identity. The repetition of the word or phrase (in your mind usually) provides an extra layer of cognitive removal from the immediate situation, allowing for more self-awareness and objectivity, so you are less likely to behave in a predetermined fashion that reinforces existing identities. Essentially, the mantra will help redirect and remind you of your intention to not fall prey to assumptions. They can help you to live more intentionally.

A personal mantra can be anything, from a single sound or word to an entire song or pledge. It can even be a physical action. A mantra just has to be effective at catching your attention and directing it toward your intent. Only you can know what that might be. In moments when I find myself on the edge of either assumption or confusion, my personal mantra is the question "What is it?" For some reason, I find this effective at calling my attention to the fact that I am missing something in the experience I'm having. It makes me look harder, trying to discern what is actually happening rather than what I believe might be happening. I try to determine what greater forces are at play beyond the individuals immediately involved in the experience. I don't always figure it out, but I often realize that there are multiple legitimate interpretations of what's happening, and this usually has a calming effect on me, because I realize the motivations that I fear are behind the situation are unlikely to be the actual motivations there. In essence, a mantra can provide just enough emotional insulation from situations to enable you to guide those situations away from becoming harmful to those involved. Then coexistence and cooperation are possible.

Incidentally, though mantras can be very effectively employed in moments of heightened tension, they certainly shouldn't be reserved exclusively for such moments. In fact, they can have a more powerful impact if you integrate them into your daily life. If you have time, it's good to make your mantra part of a recurring routine. Make it a ritual. Perhaps you are already on the verge of doing so. For example, exercise such as running functions this way for many people, enabling them to focus attention on breathing and the rhythm of their bodies in motion, clearing the mind of unhealthy preoccupations. If you already have a daily or weekly activity that soothes you, try practicing it with the intentional, enhanced focus I have been describing here.

Practice!

If you already have a mantra, what is it and how does it work for you? If you don't already have one, what are some potential options that might work for you?

Audience Awareness

In terms of identity, everyone is someone's enemy, and everyone is their own hero. Because identities are formed in contrast to other identities, the process usually leads to this antagonistic conclusion. The identity that is the inverse reflection of your own is often perceived as trying to negate your identity. This accounts for the perplexingly irrational behavior one often witnesses between otherwise sane adults who identify with sports teams that are historic rivals. Heated debates and even physical altercations are not uncommon between fans whose lives might otherwise appear nearly identical with the exception of this one difference in their identities. A fear lurks within them that they will somehow be negated by the other, if they don't violently reject it. Sports fanaticism might be an extreme example of identity antagonism, but it is only different by degrees from other forms of even more common identity discrimination.

    Fortunately, identity is navigable, even between historic rivals, if one practices what, in the ancient discipline of Rhetoric, is known as "audience awareness." What audience awareness essentially boils down to is studying the identities of those you are hoping to persuade, in order to better understand their concerns and priorities. One can then appeal to those concerns and priorities when attempting to influence the behavior of that group. For example, in an effort to build a community solar array, you would likely want to structure your argument differently for members of the chamber of commerce than you would for members of the local park improvement committee. With one you might address long-term cost-savings and energy independence, while with the other you might emphasize responsible environmental stewardship as a motivating factor.

For identity detox purposes, we will take this notion of audience awareness one step further. Instead of looking outward at those with whom we interact, often from a position of assumed neutrality, we should practice looking at ourselves from the position of our audience. We can never know exactly what others are thinking, but we can make some fairly educated guesses based on the history of interactions between different identity groups. With this added awareness of the interactive dynamic between our identities, we are much more likely to negotiate outcomes that are beneficial to both identities.

For example, if I completely ignore how I will likely be perceived by my audience and I approach the chamber of commerce with my hair down, wearing flip flops and a tie-died T-shirt, I will have immediately made my own job more difficult. If I unwittingly find myself in a Viking bar wearing green and gold, I would best be prepared to quickly identify a common bond between myself and my new audience, which is probably watching every move I make and will invariably select a representative to confront me, as long as I don't immediately leave, which would be too cowardly an act to commit. The solution: Go NFC North, the toughest division in the NFL!

In other words, your audience is only half of the equation. You are the other half. Unless you are a member of their identity group, the nature of your audience will shift perceptibly as soon as you enter their presence. What kind of chemical reaction can realistically be expected to be taking place in the minds of your audience when you are added to the mix? Are they right about you? Do they misunderstand you? Do you misunderstand them? Answering these questions is the first step toward an actual, meaningful dialogue. In fact, when I taught at Central State University, an all-Black college, I had to begin each semester with an open discussion of these types of questions, so my students could "figure me out" and come to trust me enough to learn from me… and to educate me as well.

When I lived in Lebanon, I came to realize that the American identity assigned to me included the traits of naivety, impatience, and arrogance, in addition to sincerity and diligence. This is apparently a common stereotype for Americans abroad, and one that, unfortunately, I have seen reinforced by many of my fellow expatriates. These are not inherent character traits we coincidentally share. They are aspects of mainstream American culture that become prominently visible when expressed within the context of other cultures.

In the American context, because of the deeply ingrained narrative of frontier settlement, variations of these traits are actually encouraged, but under positive guises familiar to members of that culture: naivety becomes idealism or optimism, a belief in the inevitability of progress; impatience becomes efficiency or industriousness; and arrogance becomes confidence or independence. However, in societies that place greater value on social cohesion, often those that have also been ravaged by the "progress" of modernism, these traits are likely to be interpreted as their more threatening variants. Becoming aware of how this preconceived identity influenced the way Lebanese interpreted my behavior helped me to more effectively navigate Lebanese culture, primarily by consciously practicing greater patience and humility. My idealism was already tempered with the alloy of cynicism, so naivety wasn't a significant obstacle for me to overcome.

 In short, recognizing how our assigned dominant identities are perceived by members of other identity groups is crucial for a greater understanding of the actual nature of the identities we perform and the historic underpinnings of those identities. Of course, it's unlikely that you will be able to ascertain how your identity is interpreted by others while remaining within the comfortable bubble of your own culture. The best way to do so is to ask a friend or acquaintance in that other culture to honestly explain to you how members of your identity group are commonly perceived by members of theirs. Listen closely and openly to their answer, asking as many follow-up questions as necessary for you to understand why your group is perceived that way.

Audience Awareness 2.0

The act of reversing the camera and aiming it back at ourselves, from the point-of-view of other identity groups, is so important that it's worth taking the exercise from the previous chapter a step further. In this chapter, I'll suggest a way to go deeper into our self-reflection, to reap greater benefit from it. This exercise will be more emotionally demanding than the previous one but be assured that all the prior exercises you have completed thus far in this book have prepared you for it.

One of my favorite lines of "English" poetry is from Robert Burns' "To a Louse," which is written in the Scottish Habbie dialect (a linguistic hotbed of identity conflict worthy of a book of its own). The line is "O wad some Power the giftie gie us / To see oursels as ithers see us!" (O would some Power the gift give us / To see ourselves as others see us!). The poem is mostly addressed to the parasitic insect that the speaker sees on a proud young woman's bonnet, but toward the end of the poem, he directs his speech toward the young woman, in particular, and humanity, in general, opining that we could avoid a lot of mistakes and "foolish notions" if we were able to set aside our habitual self-perceptions and instead access the perceptions that others have of us. Fortunately, such a thing is not impossible to do, but it is difficult and sometimes painful... and necessary, if one is going to practice identity detoxification.

As with most of the exercises in this book, I recommend doing this one repeatedly, with variations in the details. First, I would imagine myself in a certain setting (a familiar one is best), and then I would imagine myself being "judged" by members of at least three different identity groups in that same setting, making note of how those theoretical individuals would possibly perceive me, based on everything I know about the historic interactions of the identities being invoked, including, hopefully, actual conversations I've had with members of those groups. I would make note of the similarities and differences of those perceptions and how accurate they may or may not be regarding my actual behavior.

One variation of the exercise would be me at work, say, in a classroom, delivering a lecture on how to conduct academic research. Three identities that would likely be in any one of my classes would be a white MAGA Republican, an African American, and a Native American. How would I imagine that a stereotypical, self-identified member of each group might perceive me, a long-haired white man wearing glasses and a dress shirt? (Keep in mind that, though I am invoking stereotypes in this exercise, the intent is to expose the flaws in those stereotypes.)

Based on experiences I've had, I would imagine that the MAGA Republican might take one look at me and begin flirting with the following judgements: liberal, arrogant, elitist, out-of-touch with "reality," sensitive, soft, un-American, un-Christian, "race-traitor," etc. I would imagine an African American student might be prepared, at first glance, to make the following judgements of me: intellectual, insensitive, hard, sheltered, clueless about the student's lived experience, unsympathetic (if not clueless), enforcing standards intended to erase individuality and difference, etc. And I would imagine that a Native American student might be prepared with the following judgements of me: member of an aggressive occupying force, disrespectful of Indigenous cultures, perhaps even considering them unscientific or superstitious, trying to erase those cultures and replace them with spiritually bankrupt and ecologically unsustainable notions of science, industry, and progress, etc.

I admit that judgements like this can be a lot to take in at once, even if they're only imagined. It can be overwhelming, which is why we're doing it in the relative comfort of a thought experiment rather than in the actual classroom (where it does actually happen to teachers on a regular basis).

What I would do first is to look at the variety of attitudes, contradictory, complementary, and idiosyncratic, to appreciate the fact that I'm clearly not perceived in any singular way by any groups, or by any individuals, for that matter. I represent something a bit different to everyone. That helps me to feel less claustrophobic, less trapped in any particular identity. It gives me some breathing room.

Next, I look for the judgements that seem to negate one another, such as "sensitive" and "insensitive," and "soft" and "hard." One can't be expected to reconcile perceptions about oneself that completely contradict one another. That's just not reasonable for anyone to expect of someone else. But it's good to be aware of how these different audiences might perceive you. You might need to accordingly adjust your approach to working one-on-one with individuals or with isolated identity groups who might harbor such preconceptions about you, as I suggested in the last chapter. For mixed audiences, like most public ones, we need to be prepared for more dynamic behavior.

After identifying perceptions of my dominant identity that negate one another in a mixed audience, I look for common perceptions between the groups. When I notice something like the concern about me wanting to erase the cultures of others, which is a judgment at least two of these groups might instinctively make of me, it signals something I need to take a closer look at, and when I do, I realize it's a concern that even artists have about the STEM-obsessed culture we currently live in, which has burrowed its way into even my consciousness. I remind myself I need to remain open to creativity, individuality, and forms of evidence that can be found outside laboratories and academic databases. This can help me to avoid falling prey to some "foolish notions" of truly existential proportions.

Now, I want to be particularly mindful of perceptions that are shared, in some form or another, across all the groups in my experiment, such as those associated with "arrogant," "elitist," "intellectual," "disrespectful," and "out-of-touch" or "clueless." I certainly don't feel this way about myself. Not many people do, but many people come across this way, especially in certain professions, so I need to also make a mental note to listen carefully, be patient, understand where my students are coming from, appreciate their different life experiences... Essentially, I need to make sure I'm being respectful, which, honestly, is just another way of being professional. I should also allow myself to show emotion, to share how I feel with them, to show the common courtesy of reciprocation. I should be hiding nothing. If I feel I have something that needs to remain hidden, I should get rid of it. It's baggage. I know that's hard to do sometimes, but the effort should be made, nevertheless.

Finally, at the end of this process, I would make note of those judgements that feel completely at odds with how I conduct myself on a daily basis. Those who spend time with us will eventually realize that these aspects of the stereotypes they associate with us are simply inaccurate. You don't need to defend yourself against these judgements. Simply continue acting in contradiction to them. Your actions will vindicate you.

Most importantly, I strive to always remain aware that others whom I associate with certain stereotypes will rarely act in complete accordance with those stereotypes. Their original selves will tend to deviate from stereotypes in the direction of the original selves of others, when they are revealed.

Practice!

List stereotypical traits that you suspect members of other identity groups might habitually assign to members of identity groups with which you are commonly associated. (If you're not aware of such stereotypes, ask a member of another identity group to help you with this exercise.)

Identity Dysphoria and De-roling

Imagining all the ways your dominant and secondary identities could be perceived by those around you can be a formidable exercise, especially if you are also considering all possible expectations they might have of someone they associate with those identities, the forms of prejudice they might harbor toward those identities, and reasons they might have for being suspicious of you. Keep in mind that some of these assumptions might be somewhat accurate. It is extremely important to be mindful of this possibility. If you are disturbed by any possibly accurate assumptions about any of your identities, this is an indication that you should probably be doing something to address the cause of the accuracy. Nevertheless, many of the assumptions about you, based on your perceived identities, will simply be wrong, as are many of your assumptions of others.

    If you really dig into the previous audience awareness and camera-reversal exercises, being perfectly honest with yourself, particularly regarding the fallacious assumptions about your character, at some point you might even gain a small sense of what gender dysphoria feels like: the feeling of being trapped within an imposed identity that doesn't remotely resemble how you feel about yourself. Though it is an enlightening experience, it can also be traumatizing. It takes strength to face some of these realizations, but it is an endeavor we must make, if we are to take control of our collective narrative.

Fortunately, if you perform the exercise in its entirety, there are emotionally uplifting aspects to it as well. Don't forget to also recognize ways in which you might be admired or appreciated by others based on your imposed identities, particularly if there is some accuracy to those assumptions. Also, don't forget to recognize secondary identities associated with those around you, and consider how many of those other identities you share with them. You always have something in common with everyone around you, even if it is simply being an Earthling, which is not an identity to be taken lightly.

The fact that you actually embody many identities, as discussed in "The Mansion of Yourself," leads us to another exercise you can practice to counteract any negative side effects that might result from the audience awareness exercise described in the previous chapter. It is often practiced by abuse counselors, who are routinely exposed to the traumatic narratives of their clients and unavoidably internalize those narratives as part of their role as counselors. It is also practiced by actors who have been asked to play the roles of characters with unhealthy psychological conditions. These professionals understand that they perform many roles in their lives, and when they begin to feel overwhelmed by the psychological state of one of those roles they know that it is time to "de-role." They need to take a break from that particular role and inhabit one of their other roles.

A counselor might take a break between clients to call her daughter and embody her role as a mother. An actor might take a break from his role as a murderer to call his girlfriend and be a lover. If you begin to feel oppressed by the weight of expectations and assumptions about a particular identity of yours, consciously set that role aside and more deeply inhabit another one of your roles, one that you find comforting or revitalizing or perhaps simply more aligned with one of the secondary identities of those around you. Imagine the common challenges and rewards you experience. This should bump you out of most negative identity feedback loops in which you might find yourself.

Cracking Your Binary Code

The trend in Western civilization over the past several centuries has been toward a greater binarism in our thinking. What I mean by this is that we have been increasingly more inclined to divide the world into halves, along the lines of the oppositions used as examples in the "Mind Over Metaphor" chapter (good and bad, light and dark, male and female, etc.), whereby everything in existence falls to one side or the other of the divide, and usually one side of the binary is preferred over the other. In fact, in the most orthodox manifestation of binary thought, everything in existence is either good or bad. Fortunately, this kind of thinking is by no means universal. For example, outside of cultures highly influenced by monotheism, people tend to have more flexible approaches to the interpretation of reality. Uncertainty regarding the ultimate value of things is more tolerated.

    I do not claim to have privileged knowledge of the true nature of reality, but I do know that the nature of human knowledge, as well as human identity, which is, after all, a form of knowledge, resembles "Zeno's paradox" far more than it resembles any binary model of the world. According to the ancient Greek philosopher Zeno, there are an infinite number of points between any two points, no matter how close those two might be to one another, because the distance between any two points can always be halved. If we think of these points as positions that one might take on an issue, or as simply vantage points, we are provided with a convenient, and, I believe, accurate metaphor. The possible legitimate positions on any given subject are far more than two.

Another way of more accurately modeling the historic, lived experience of human knowledge is by way of a "dialectical" process, one that works through opposition and synthesis. Perhaps the best description of this process was provided by the 19th century German philosopher Georg Hegel, so it is sometimes referred to as "Hegel's dialectic." In this process, when an idea, or "thesis," is presented, almost invariably an opposition to that idea emerges, an "antithesis." That's where it would end, if we lived in a binary universe, but that's never where it actually ends. There's struggle and debate and change. Eventually, a third position arises, usually at the point where Zeno would bisect the distance between the two initial positions, and a third idea arises, often a synthesis of the thesis and antithesis.

This new idea then becomes the thesis to which a new antithesis arises, and the process continues. So, for example, out of the epic ideological struggle between Communism and Capitalism arose the third point of Social Democracy, which has become the thesis to which a new antithesis seems to be arising (Capitalist Oligarchy?), and between the two a new synthesis will eventually arise. Ad infinitum! Well, until the end of human civilization, at least.

Whether or not you buy this metaphoric representation of the history of human ideas, it does present us with another effective exercise for clearing the mind of prejudice. It sounds simple in theory, but, like a good Zen koan, it can occupy you nearly endlessly in practice. The exercise is designed to counteract your preprogrammed binary assumptions about the world, utilizing your ingrained psychological grammar.

What you do is simply take an either/or statement that feels fairly uncontestable to you and turn it into an and/and statement, and then figure out how it could be true as an and/and statement. "It is either light or it is dark" becomes "It is light and it is dark." "It is cold or it is hot" becomes "It is cold and it is hot." "You can either be for X or against X" becomes "You can be for and against X." Like I said, the possibilities are nearly endless, and, almost without fail, you will find the and/and explanations to be far more profound and capital-T-true than the either/or explanations. By the way, if this approach reminds you of Keats' "negative capability," you're absolutely correct. Hegel and Keats were drawing water from the same well.

Practice!

List as many either/or statements as you can think of, and turn them into and/and statements. Then imagine the ways in which these new and/and statements could be True.

Talking to Others

Humans are meant to communicate. It's how we became so adaptable, by replacing instinct with imagination and communication. Once we developed the ability to produce a mental image of things not physically before us, things distant in space or time, and found ways to talk about those things, we held the key to conscious adaptation... to strategy and education. Also, as one of the only eusocial vertebrates, with a level of social organization matched only by insects such as ants or bees, communication serves as the foundation of that structure. Even extreme introverts feel the need to talk to someone once in a while. However, this powerful tool begins working against us when we lock ourselves into particular identity groups and communicate exclusively with members of those groups. Our ability to achieve defamiliarization and innovation diminishes exponentially. We become locked into a particular worldview that is necessarily only a partial view of the actual world. We run the risk of becoming incapable of imagining why anyone would live a life any different than our own.

So, if we are committed to recalibrating our identities to better align with the existing world, what we need to do is talk to "others." We need to leave our cultural comfort zones and engage with people we wouldn't habitually engage with. This doesn't mean you necessarily need to go very far to do so. Though you might decide to physically visit an alien environment, as I suggested you do imaginatively in the "Re-setting Yourself" chapter, it's very likely that you can simply talk to a neighbor you've never spoken to before. Talk to a coworker, an employee, preferably someone you perceive as being a member of a different identity group.

Engage them in conversation. In other words, 1) ask them a question, perhaps for advice; 2) carefully listen to their answer; 3) form another question based on their initial response; 4) carefully listen to their new answer; 5) share any personal information that you feel is relevant to the subject, such as the reason for your question or challenges you face regarding the subject; 6) continue in this manner as long as the other participant seems interested in the subject, allowing them to change the subject while you listen. Most people feel flattered by a sincere request to know something about their expertise or about their feelings on a subject. That alone is progress, but you are also likely to learn something you didn't know before, which will add to the store of knowledge that informs your own sense of self and its relation to a now slightly bigger world.

Here's one more wrinkle I'd like to add to this exercise: talk to yourself more often. I realize that such behavior is stigmatized throughout much of the West but be assured that you will not go crazy if you talk to yourself. You're already doing it unconsciously all the time. Making it more intentional, even if you're doing it silently, in your head, can be an effective method for gaining distance from dominant identities that have been assigned to you. In essence, by treating yourself as an other and practicing the conversational method outlined above, you gain a greater appreciation for the difference between your self and your identity. You will likely find that the self is the one asking questions of the identity, since the self preexists the prejudices and assumptions that provide ready answers for the identity. If you question far enough, the identity will often run out of answers, leaving you with the truth. Another reason to do this exercise is because you are an other to everyone else, so consciously experiencing yourself as an other helps you understand how everyone else experiences you.

Sometimes Love Is the Greatest Challenge

When we have identified a person, or a group of people, as being dangerous or beneath contempt, the thought of extending our love to them can seem to be the most impossible thing imaginable. Being able to lift an automobile off the ground with your bare hands seems a more likely possibility. Nevertheless, as hard as it might seem, it is possible for us to love our enemies. As a Black minister once said to me, regarding someone who was criticizing her, "I might not like him, but, as a Christian, I love him." Regardless of our religious beliefs, if we are serious about detoxifying our identities, we must also adopt this practice.

It's important to keep in mind that we don't do this for some ethereal, kumbaya moment that provides a sense of unity with only other likeminded people. We should do this because hatred clouds judgement terribly and causes people to misinterpret and exaggerate the intentions of others and to preemptively or excessively strike out against perceived threats, which leads the other side to do the same, escalating perceived conflicts into actual conflicts. If we know that we are capable of loving one another, we are able to think more clearly and rationally about our intentions toward one another. The blinding grip of fear and anger releases us.

One of the best ways to cultivate this capacity is through this simple, though admittedly difficult, exercise: 1) visualize, or look at an actual image of, the person you hate, or a representative of the group you hate, and 2) repeat to yourself, out loud or in your head, as though you mean it, "I love you," over and over, until your initial revulsion subsides. Depending on the intensity of your dislike for the object of this meditation, you may have to do it for quite some time, possibly over many sessions, before your hatred begins to diminish and is replaced by something resembling love, but it will happen if you put in the effort. Psychologists assure us that if you go through the motions long enough with anything, you will eventually believe in what you are saying or doing, if for no other reason than because it has become a habit.

    Do not worry that you will suddenly excuse any unjust behavior on the other's part, or that you will suddenly become like them. That's not how it works with people you have formerly hated. When you open yourself to them, they don't rush inside and take over. On the contrary, you will gain greater mental clarity and control over your own behavior, because you won't be constantly acting in instinctive opposition to everything they do. They will lose their power to define your response to their actions. It is very liberating. The conventional cultural contrast between love and reason is a false contrast. Love is the purest manifestation of reason.

Letting Go

Of course, whenever you feel that an unwanted identity is being imposed upon you or someone else, you should speak up and speak out. Explain what you perceive to be happening. If you are the aggrieved party, explain your actual position, your chosen role, your real identity. The situation will not change if you don't.

However, sometimes the situation will still not change. Sometimes people simply won't believe you, or there will be so many people assuming things about you that you would have to spend nearly every moment of every day explaining yourself to others. I wish this were not so, but I know it is a reality for some. If this isn't the case for you, please understand that it is for some others, and listen to them. If this is the case for you, please try to not let it deter you from the goals you had when you were a child, the dreams you allow yourself to entertain in those moments when you feel free of imposed identity. Practice letting go of the assumptions others have about you. Carry on with your higher ambitions.

We are all born into history, with certain roles readymade for us. We cannot escape that particular fate. However, consistent action toward your highest goal, even if that goal is not achieved within your lifetime, will influence the history into which others are born. And sometimes, to do that, we need to stop caring about what others think of us. When you're already swimming against a current, that amount of extra drag can simply be too much. Let it go.

Conclusion: The Limits of Objectivity

We cannot choose to be uninvolved in history. We can't step into the background, whatever its color might be, and pretend we aren't here. By simply existing, we are involved. We are part of everyone else's stories. Even as a bystander, we are a witness, an audience to whatever unfolds. If we witness an injustice and do nothing, we are that person who witnessed an injustice and did nothing. We will be that person as long as our name can be found in human records. We will continue to be that person long after death. If we run away, we will be the one who ran away. And if we are one who tried conscientiously to leave the world a better place than we found it, then that is who we will be, even if we made a few mistakes here and there.

We can change the way we interpret history, but we can't change what actually happened, the actuality of which can never be erased, for it is the animating spirit of history… as long as history itself exists. As long as we live within a human society, we can neither extricate ourselves from the identities history assigned us at birth nor the ongoing narratives in which those identities are implicated. But, within the freedom of our imaginations, we can approximate our mental state before we were indoctrinated into those identities, and from that state we can better see our priorities for what they are. This is the closest we can get to "objectivity." From this vantage, we can better see what societal purpose our priorities are serving, and then we can assume the agency to make revisions to the narrative going forward, one attitude at a time, one interaction at a time, one life at a time.

Modern physics informs us that nothing in the universe can exist in isolation from the rest of the universe. All things are interconnected through the act of quantum entanglement. As soon as two particles have interacted, they influence each other's behavior henceforth... and all other particles with which they interact for perpetuity, even light years apart. Not even the subatomic components of our beings will allow us to stand apart from others. We are bound to one another as ineluctably as fate... but it is a fate we can choose to influence.

You have just finished a journey in ideas and self-exploration. What conclusions have you drawn from it? What questions remain that you would like to ask me and others who have read the book? Please share:

Further Study

The ideas and techniques presented in this book have been inspired by the work of many others, literally from everything I have studied and experienced over the past 30 years of my life striving to be a better poet. Identifying every source would be impossible. However, there are a few that come immediately to mind as having been particularly eye-opening for me at various times in the past, so I will offer them here, in case you would like to further explore some of the likely influences for the approaches discussed in this book.

    I have absorbed quite a bit from the philosophical and spiritual traditions of Taoism, Buddhism, Gnosticism, Transcendentalism, and Pragmatism, particularly from the writings of Thich Nhat Hanh, Shunryu Suzuki, Charlotte Beck, Robert Aitken, Martin Buber, Ralph Waldo Emerson, Margaret Fuller, William James, Richard Rorty, and Cornel West, as well as from the writings of mystics from nearly every religion, whom it can be said have often practiced the same Perennial Faith. Regarding the influence of language and narrative on identity, I have benefited tremendously from the work of Kenneth Burke, Paul Ricoeur, Jacques Lacan, George Lakoff, Mark Johnson, Mark Turner, Arnold Ludwig and Dan McAdams. I've likewise benefited from the interdisciplinary work of Mary Bateson, Mihaly Csikszentmihalyi, George Herbert Mead, Carl Rogers, Julian Jaynes, Jean Liedloff, Denis Wood, E.O. Wilson,

Walter Benjamin, Blackwolf Jones, Kate Soper, and Wendell Berry. From Frederick Douglass, Martin Luther King, Jr, Malcom X, James Baldwin, Richard Wright, Ralph Ellison, Vine Deloria, Jr, bell hooks, Judith Butler, Edward Said, and Claudia Rankine. I have gained much insight into the historic construction and lived reality of racial and gendered identity. Amin Maalouf's *On Identity* was particularly eye-opening for me, regarding the macrocosmic, geopolitical importance of understanding identity. I have likewise gained insights from the guided practice of both Zen and Yoga meditation.

It's probably not surprising to learn that one of the greatest influences for me has been poetry, every kind of poetry I could get my hands on, from the English-language tradition as well as from many other language traditions (in translation mostly). The prose of poets has been tremendously important for me as well, with the writings of the Romantics figuring prominently in my mind, particularly those of Keats and Coleridge, with their keen insights into the nature of human imagination. The prose of T.S. Eliot, Wallace Stevens, Denise Levertov, and Adrienne Rich impressed upon me the nature of the relationship between poetry and society, and the responsibilities incumbent upon poets in any age. Again, I strongly encourage you to read poetry, all kinds of poetry. Don't worry if you don't "get it." It's working, even when you don't know how it's working. In fact, it's better if you don't completely understand what it's doing. Remember to cultivate mystery in your life, so you may continue to find new rooms in the mansion of your self.

Finally, if you are interested in learning more about the scientific study of unconscious bias and its effects on individuals and on society, there are a number of good books that approach the subject from the perspective of Social Psychology. Here are a few that might be good places to start: *Whistling Vivaldi*, by Claude Steele; *Everyday Bias*, by Howard Ross; *Blindspot*, by Mahzarin Banaji and Anthony Greenwald; and *The Person You Mean to Be*, by Dolly Chugh.

Acknowledgements

I'd like to thank the following individuals for encouraging me to continue working on what initially seemed a strange endeavor, as well as those who provided me with feedback on the work at various stages in the research and writing process: Kamal Abu Husayn, Flore Chevaillier, Karen Croftcheck, Rula Diab, Gloria Eslinger, Justina Gemignani, Trisha Hanson, Kenna Bolton Holz, Mark Horan, Gregory Klassen, Marsha Lue, Charlie Lydon, Ephraim Nikoi, Opolot Okia, John Paul, Brooke Suddeth, Bryan Tomasovich, Matthew Tredinnick, and Jade Wong. Thank you all for your insight and generosity. I'd also like to thank all the students who have taken my Language, Narrative, and Unconscious Bias course over the years—it was for you that I originally began this work.

About the Author

Jayson Iwen is the author of *Roze & Blud*, which won the Miller Williams Poetry Prize and was a finalist for the National Poetry Series. He's also the author of *Gnarly Wounds*, *A Momentary Jokebook*, which won the Ruthanne Wiley Memorial Novella Contest, and *Six Trips in Two Directions*, winner of the Emergency Press International Book Contest. His poetry, prose, and translations have appeared in numerous journals, including *Diagram*, *Fence*, *New American Writing*, *Nimrod*, *Pleiades*, *Third Coast*, *Tikkun*, *Water~Stone*, and *World Literature Today*. His work has been nominated for The Pushcart Prize several times. He lives in the Twin Ports, where he teaches in the Writing and Public Leadership programs at The University of Wisconsin – Superior, where he won the 2023 Students' Choice for Outstanding Teaching Award.

Made in the USA
Columbia, SC
05 March 2024